Mr. Native 원서 읽기

스티븐 C. 런딘 외 지음 | 유동익 해설

Mr. Native 원서 읽기 FISH!

퍼   냄   2007년 12월 20일 1판 1쇄 박음 • 2007년 12월 25일 1판 1쇄 퍼냄

지 은 이   스티븐 C. 런딘 외

해   설   유동익

퍼 낸 이   김철종

퍼 낸 곳   (주)한언
          등록번호 제1-128호 / 등록일자 1983. 9. 30

주   소   서울시 마포구 신수동 63-14 구 프라자 6층(우 121-854)
          TEL. 02-701-6616(대) / FAX. 02-701-4449

책임편집   윤혜영 hyyun@haneon.com

디 자 인   양진규 jkyang@haneon.com

홈페이지   **www.haneon.com**

e-mail   haneon@haneon.com

ISBN   978-89-5596-448-6 03740

Mr. Native 원서 읽기

Fish!

by stephen C. Lundin, Harry Paul, and John Christensen

Catch the Energy
&
Release the Potential

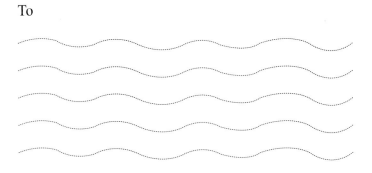

To

From

ᏗᏗ 원서를 읽어야 하는 이유

영어 공부 잘하는 비결?

직장인들에게 영어 공부는 평생 떠안고 가야 할 숙제다. 중학교부터 대학교까지 10년 넘게 영어를 해왔지만 듣기와 말하기는 커녕 읽기조차 쉽지 않다. 도대체 왜 영어는 정복되지 않는 걸까? 사람들은 읽다가 이해가 안 되어 막히면 읽기를 포기해버린다. 하지만 당신 혼자 그러는 것이 아니니 너무 의기소침해할 필요는 없다. 읽기는 누구에게나 어려우니까.

그렇다면 어떻게 해야 할까? 개인마다 차이는 있겠지만 과연 얼마나 '영어를 즐기고 시간과 열정을 쏟았느냐'에 달려 있다. 여기에 구체적인 팁 몇 가지를 알려주겠다.

1. 자신의 수준에 맞는 글을 읽어라. 남들 읽는다고 해서 영자신문이나 두껍고 어려운 책을 읽을 필요가 없다.

2. 읽는 중간에 사전을 찾기 위해 멈추지 마라. 그러면 문맥의 흐름을 놓치게 되고 이해의 정도도 떨어지게 된다.

3. 단어 순서대로 읽어라. 우리말로 바꿔서 해석을 하려고 하는 순간 영어는 어려워진다. 그냥 영어 어순 그대로 읽고 이해해라.

4. 본인에게 필요한 정보, 재미있어 할 만한 글을 찾아라. 그러면 스스로 자연스럽게 동기부여가 될 것이다.

인내를 가지고 오랫동안 꾸준한 열정을 보여줄 때 영어를 읽는 눈, 듣는 귀, 말하는 입은 선물처럼 주어진다.

직장인들을 위한 안성맞춤형 주제와 난이도!

많은 사람들이 원서를 읽겠다고 마음먹고 책을 펼쳐들었다가도 모르는 단어나 해석하기 어려운 문장을 만나면 중간에 읽기를 포기하곤 한다. 영어 공부를 위해 원서를 고를 때는 주제와 난이도를 꼼꼼히 따져봐야 한다. 어휘의 난이도가 과연 나의 수준에 맞는지, 주제가 너무 딱딱하거나 혹은 유치하지 않은지 말이다. 이런 전제조건이 충족되지 않으면 한 문장 한 문장 읽어나가기가 힘겨워지고 학습효과는 기대할 수 없다.

이 책은 직장인 독자들이 관심을 가져야 할 자기계발이나 처세와 관련된 내용이다. 회사 업무 효율을 높이고 행복하게 일할 수 있도록 도와주는 재미있고 실용적인 내용이 펼쳐질 것이다. 그리고 막히는 부분이 없이 단숨에 읽을 수 있도록 오른쪽 페이지에는 원문을, 왼쪽 페이지에는 단어 설명과 문장 해설을 배치하였다. 이야기의 흐름이 끊기지 않도록 배려한 것이다. 또 중간 중간에 미국에서도 바로 써먹을 수 있는 회화 표현을 실었다. 마지막에는 한글 요약문을 실어 본문의 내용을 확인할 수 있도록 했다.

당신의 삶에 활력을 불어넣는 Fish!

이 책은 일과 삶에 열정을 불러오는 방법에 관한 경영 우화이다. 성실한 금융회사의 관리자 메리 제인은 '유독성 폐기물 더미'라는 골칫덩이 부서를 떠맡게 된다. 이때 메리 제인 앞에 세계적인 '파이크 플레이스 어시장'과 시장상인 로니가 나타난다. 그리고 커리어우먼 메리 제인과 쾌활한 시장상인 로니는 '유독성 폐기물 더미'를 변화시키기 위한 프로젝트를 시작한다. 이들의 좌충우돌 유쾌한 성공 스토리 속에 녹아 있는 4가지 FISH! 철학이 당신의 일과 삶에 활력을 불어 넣어줄 것이다.

한국어판으로 출간되어 20만 명이 넘는 국내 독자의 사랑을 받았던 FISH!를 이제 원서 그대로 만나볼 수 있다.

Professional Endorsements
for FISH!

"Not only is FISH! a great story in its own right—told in an engaging and thought-provoking way—but the business lessons it teaches are sure to improve any organization that takes the time to apply them. Catch the wave!"

— PETER ISLER AND PETER ECONOMY,
author of At the Helm:
Business Lessons for
Navigating Rough Waters

"Fish! is not just a book about business or boosting morale and motivating employees. It's a book about Life. It's a book about how we should live our daily life and how we interact with family members, friends, and people we meet on the street. By using what you'll learn in the book, you will not only become a better manager, you'll become a better person, and that's far more important."

— RICHARD SULPIZIO,
president and chief operating officer of Qualcomm

"Lundin, Paul, and Christensen know the right formula for teaching principles that improve conditions in the workplace: Tell a good story! Fish! is perfectly suited for teaching four powerful principles that form the bedrock of a successful company. I recommend their book to anymore, on any level, who wants to make a difference at work."

– HYRUM SMITH,
co-chairman of Franklin Covey Company

"I find myself energized by the message and clearly see the potential of applying the concepts throughout our 15,000-person organization. The author's 'catch the energy and release the potential' truly captures the essence of this fine book and its message."

– DONALD D. SNYDER,
president of Boyd Gaming Corporation

"This book points out in a very clever and compelling manner that being a good manager of people is not much more than using common sense and the 'Golden Rule'— treat others the way you would like to be treated."

– ROBERT J. NUGENT,
president and CEO of FOODMAKER, Inc. (Jack in the box)

Dedication

This book is for the millions of workers who relish the thought of having a more playfully productive atmosphere at work and for the billions of fish who would rather not find themselves flying through the air at the world famous Pike Place Fish market.

Enclosed are the keys to creating an innovative and accountable work environment where a playful, attentive, and engaging attitude leads to more energy, enthusiasm, productivity, and creativity.

foreword 저자 이외의 사람이 쓰는 서문(저자가 쓰는 서문은 preface라고 한다)
incredible 놀라운 **catch on film** 화면에 담다 **illustrate** 설명하다 **Gung
Ho!** 중국어 공화(工和)에서 유래한 단어로 '무한한 열정과 에너지'라는 뜻(켄
플렌차드의 베스트셀러 제목) **ignite** 불을 붙이다, 흥분시키다 **workforce** 전 직
원, 노동력 **Raving Fans** 열광하는 팬(켄 플렌차드의 베스트셀러 제목) **colleague** 동료 **team up (with)** ~와 협력하다 **fabulous** 멋진 **fulfillment** 성취
work-related 일과 관련된 **get ready for** 준비하다 **travel to work** 일하러
가다 **contemplate** 심사숙고하다

• • •

**When we choose to love...we can catch our limit of happiness...every
day** catch는 보통 '붙잡다' 정도의 뜻으로 쓰이지만 여기서는 '경험하다' 즉,
'행복의 한계를 경험하다'로 해석할 수 있다.

• • •

How long is soon?
곧 이면 언제를 말하는 거야?

미국은 바쁘게 돌아가는 동적인 사회이다. 따라서 미국인들은 자신들의 시간
을 철저하게 관리하는 습관을 가지고 있다. 직장에서도 상사는 일의 진척을 시
간단위로 묻는 경우가 많다. 직장에서 될 수 있는 대로 업무만 하고 잡담(small
talk)은 피하는 것도 그러한 이유 때문이다. 한 마디로 철저하게 '일할 때는 일
하고 놀 때는 놀자'라는 생각을 가지고 있다(Work while you work, play while
you play).

Foreword

by Ken Blanchard, Ph.D.,

co-author of The One Minute Manager,

Raving Fans, and Gung Ho!

Fish! is an incredible story that John Christensen first caught on film. he and his company, ChartHouse, produced an amazing video on the world famous Pike Place Fish market in Seattle. I have been showing this video at every one of my seminars to illustrate what happens when you create Gung Ho! employees—you ignite your workplace and create Raving Fans®.

Now Stephen Lundin, and long-term colleague of mine Harry Paul, have teamed up with John to bring the Fish! story to print. In whatever media it appears, it's a fabulous love story. As the book suggests, "When we choose to love the work we do, we can catch our limit of happiness, meaning, and fulfillment every day."

How important is that? Incredibly important, especially when you consider that people spend about 75 percent of their adult wake time doing work-related activities—getting ready for work, travelling to work, working, contemplating

decompress 긴장이 풀리다 share with 공유하다 implement 실행하다, 수
단 strategy 전략 guarantee 보증하다 benefit 이익 retention 유지 take
pride in ~을 자랑스럽게 여기다 make a difference 변화를 만들다 philosophy 철학 prevent 방지하다 burnout 소모, 극도의 피로 marvelous 놀
라운, 믿기 어려운

· · ·

And yet, too many people are trading time on the job to satisfy needs
elsewhere '그러나 여전히 많은 사람들이 현재의 직장이 아닌 또 다른 곳에서
욕구를 충족시키기 위해 시간을 낭비하고 있다' trade on은 '악용하다'라는
의미를 갖는다.
Share it with everyone with whom you work 'Share it with everyone'과
'You work with them'을 결합한 관계대명사 문장이다.
increase employee retention 이 문장을 해석하면 '종업원들을 다른 곳으로
옮기지 않게 한다'는 뜻이다.

work, and decompressing after work. If we spend that much time in that part of our lives, we ought to enjoy it and be energized by it. And yet, too many people are trading time on the job to satisfy of life for many people.

Those days can stop now—if you read Fish!, share it with everyone with whom you work, and implement the four secrets and suggested strategies that Lundin, Paul, and Christensen give you. I guarantee that every manger will benefit from Fish!, because it will not only increase employee retention, it will motivate people to take pride in what they do. People like to work in an environment that is fun, energizing, and where they can make a difference. The Fish! philosophy will also benefit every employee, because it prevents burnout and will keep you excited about what you do.

As you can tell, I'm excited about Fish! I think this is a marvelous book. The story of the world famous Pike Place Fish market is fantastic. But this book is not just about selling fish; it's a love story that can happen in your organization, too.

fashionable 유행의 settle for ~을 받아들이다, 정착하다 poetry 시(詩)
sailboat 범선 quest 탐색 chase 추격하다, 뒤쫓다 significant 의미심장한,
중요한 responsibility 책임 calling 소명 make visible 눈에 보이다, 명백한
literally 문자 그대로 a new line of work 새로운 직장 parable 우화, 비유
invent 창조하다 source 근원, 출처

• • •

It is fashionable ... We should not settle for anything less than doing
what we love '어떤 곳에 정착하기보다는 스스로 사랑하는 일을 해야 한다'
여기서 not A less than B는 'A라기보다는 B이다'는 뜻이다.

For others, a true calling hasn't made itself visible yet. '다른 사람들에게
진실된 소명 그 자체는 아직 보이지 않는다'

16

Loving What You Do

It is fashionable today to believe that we should not settle for anything less than doing what we love. Write poetry, travel the world on a sailboat, paint—to whatever you love, and the money will follow. We tell ourselves that life is too short to spend our working hours doing anything less than the ideal, and we continue our search for the perfect workplace. The danger is that if our quest for ideal work focuses us on the future, we will miss the amazingly wonderful life that is available today, in this moment.

The fact is that in the real world there are conditions which prevent us from chasing the perfect, ideal job. many of us have significant responsibilities to family members or to a way of life. For others, a true calling hasn't made itself visible yet. Some of us are under so much stress in our personal lives there is literally no time or energy to seek a new line of work.

Fish! is a parable, an invented story about finding the deep source of energy, creativity, and passion that exists inside each of us by learning to love what we do, even if at the moment we may not be doing exactly what we love.

Contents

dreary 쓸쓸한, 음울한 **dismal** 음침한 우울한 **meteorologist** 기상학자
retrace 되돌아가다, 근원을 찾다 **relocate** 다시 배치하다, 이동시키다

・・・

The best the meteorologist on Channel 4 could offer was a possible break in clouds around noon. '채널 4번의 기상학자가 말한 가장 좋은 내용은 정오 경 구름이 걷힐 것이라는 것이었다' 이 문장의 break in clouds라는 표현을 '구름이 걷히다'라는 뜻으로 숙어처럼 기억하면 좋다.

What a roller coaster '롤러코스터를 탄 것처럼'

⌢ Seattle-Monday Morning

It was a wet, cold, dark, dreary, dismal Monday in Seattle, inside and out. The best the meteorologist on Channel 4 could offer was a possible break in the clouds around noon. On days like this Mary jane Ramirez missed Southern California.

What a roller coaster, she thought, as her mind retracted the last three years. Dan, her husband, had received a great offer from Microrule and she had been confident she could find a job once they relocated. In just

daycare 탁아소(특히 낮에 운영되는) **True to one's confidence** 기대했던 대로 **operations area** 운영부 **supervisory position** 관리직 **burst** (감정 등을) 갑작스럽게 표현하다, 폭발하다 **the advanced** 고급의 **put the children to bed** 아이들을 재우다 **talk well into the night** 저녁 늦게까지 대화를 나누다 **face** 직면하다 **anticipate** 예측하다 **contingency** 우연성, 우연의 사고 **rush** 서두르다, 돌진하다 **aneurysm** 동맥류 **genetic** 유전적인 **internal** 내부의 **oddity** 희귀함 **bleeding** 출혈 **consciousness** 의식

• • •

Their house hit the Los Angeles market just at the right time... hit the market은 원래 '(물건 등이) 시장에 나오다'라는 뜻으로 여기서는 '그들의 집이 LA의 (부동산) 시장에 제때 나오다' 정도로 해석하면 된다.

The spirit of each shined in the presence of the other. '그들 각자의 영혼은 서로의 존재로 인해 빛나고 있었다'

four short weeks they had given notice, packed, moved, and found great daycare for the kids. Their house hit the Los Angeles housing market just at the right time and sold immediately. True to her confidence, Mary Jane quickly found a supervisory position in the operations area of First Guarantee Financial, one of Seattle's largest financial institutions.

Dan really loved his job at Microrule. When he came home at night he was bursting with energy and full of stories about the great company for which he now worked and the advanced work they were doing. Dan and Mary Jane would frequently put the children to bed and talk well into the evening. As excited as Dan was about his new company, he was always just as interested in her day, wanting to know about her new colleagues and the challenges she was facing in her work life. Anyone watching would easily guess that they were best friends. The spirit of each shined in the presence of the other.

Their detailed planning had anticipated every possible contingency but one. Twelve months after moving to Seattle, Dan was rushed to the hospital with a burst aneurysm—"a genetic oddity" they called it—and he died of internal bleeding while never regaining consciousness.

surge 파도 **well up** 솟구치다 **catch oneself** 자제하다 **swamp with work** 일이 많아 눈코 뜰 새 없다 **reputation** 명성, 평판 **supervisor** 관리자, 감독 관 **ethic** 윤리 **in-basket** 미결 서류함 **conduct** 수행하다 **pass through** 지 나가다, 거치다 **in return** 그 보답으로

· · ·

...She had a work ethic that almost always left her in-basket empty. '그 녀는 미결 서류함을 거의 늘 비워놓는 직업윤리를 가지고 있었다' 여기서 in-basket은 미결 서류함이라는 뜻으로 반대말로 out-basket이 있다. in-basket 과 out-basket을 사용하여 관라자의 결재능력을 훈련하는 것을 'In-basket method'라고 한다.

Stopping in mid-thought, with memories flooding her mind, a surge of emotion welled up inside her. 여기서 stop in은 '그만두다'라는 뜻으로 문 장을 해석하면 '생각 중간에, 기억들이 그녀의 마음으로 밀려들어오면서, 그녀 의 내부에서 감정의 파도가 솟구쳤다'

There was no warning and no time to say good-bye.

That was two years ago this month. We weren't even in Seattle a full year.

Stopping in mid-thought, with memories flooding her mind, a surge of emotion welled up inside her. She caught herself. This is not the time to think about my personal life; the workday is less than half over, and I'm swamped with work.

First Guarantee Financial

During her three years at First Guarantee, Mary Jane had developed a great reputation as a "can-do" supervisor. She wasn't the first to arrive or the last to leave, but she had a work ethic that almost always left her in-basket empty. The thoughtful way she conducted her work actually led to a small problem in the organization as others tried to make sure that their work passed through her part of the organization. They knew the work would get done on time and with the highest quality.

She was also a good person to work for. She always listened closely to the concerns and ideas of her staff and was well liked and respected in return. It wasn't uncommon

lead in ~로 끌어들이다 **cover** 떠맡다, ~을 대신하다 **easygoing** 편안한
generate 생산하다 **report** 부하직원 **associate** 동료 **in sharp contrast** 극
히 대조적으로 **unresponsive** 반응하지 않는 **entitlement** 유명무실한
zombie 무기력한 사람 **wasteland** 황무지 **swap stories** 의견교환을 하다
fiasco 대실패(오랫동안 계획된 일들이 잘못된 것) **deserve** ~할 만하다 **roar** 외
치다 **somewhat** 다소 **reluctantly** 마지못해

• • •

**Those who visited the third floor described that...it sucked the life
right out of you.** 여기서 'right out of'는 '~로부터 당장에'라는 뜻으로 전
체 문장을 해석하면 '3층을 방문한 사람들은 그곳이 당신의 삶을 당장에 빨아
들일 정도로 죽어 있는 곳이라고 묘사했다'

for her to cover for someone with a sick child or important appointment. And, as a working manager, she led her department in production. She did this in an easygoing way, which rarely generated any tension — other than tension to get the job done well. Her direct reports and associates enjoyed working with and for her. Mary Jane's small group developed a reputation as a team you could count on.

In sharp contrast, there was a large operations group on the third floor that was often the topic of conversation for the opposite reason. Words like unresponsive, entitlement, zombie, unpleasant, slow, wasteland, and negative were used frequently to describe this group.

Supervisors swapped stories about the latest fiasco on the third floor. Those who visited the third floor described it as a place so dead that it sucked the life right out of you. Mary Jane remembered the laughter when one of the other managers said that he deserved a Nobel Prize. When she asked what he meant, he said, "I think I may have discovered life on the third floor." Everyone roared.

Then, a few weeks later, Mary Jane had cautiously and somewhat reluctantly accepted a promotion to manager of the operations group on the third floor of First Guarantee.

reservation 예약, 보류 willingness 기꺼이 하는 마음 bond 유대감
acutely 날카롭게, 격렬하게 unforeseen 생각지 않은 hospitalization 입원
turn down 거절하다 infamous 불명예스러운 struggle 분투하다 mildly
부드럽게 observe 관찰하다 veteran 경험 많은

• • •

...she had major reservations about accepting the job. reservation은 보
통 '예약'이라는 뜻으로 많이 사용하지만 여기서는 '보류'라는 뜻으로 쓰였
다. 문장을 해석하면 '그녀는 그 일을 받아들이는 것을 심각하게 보류했었다'
If it hadn't been for all of the unforeseen expenses of Dan's hospitalization, she probably would have turned down the promotion. 가정법
과거완료형식의 문장이다(만일 ~하지 않았더라면, ~했었을 텐데).

• • •

It's my turn to kiss the bride
내가 신부에게 키스할 차례다

미국인들은 한국인들처럼 예식장에서 축의금을 내는 경우가 거의 없으며 부조
금을 낸다 해도 대개 가족에 한한다. 대신에 선물로 'towel, silverware, plates,
clock' 같은 것들을 가지고 간다. 결혼식이 끝나고 하객들을 맞는 연회(recep-
tion)에서는 모두 열을 지어 신랑, 신부와 악수를 하게 되는데 이때 모든 하객
들이 신부에게 키스하는 것이 미국의 관습이다.

While the company had great hopes for her, she had major reservations about accepting the job. She had been comfortable in her present job — and her willingness to take risks had been much higher before Dan's death. The group she had been supervising had been with her during the rough days after Dan's death, and she had felt a strong bond with them. It would be hard to leave people who had shared so much of themselves during such dark times.

Mary Jane was acutely aware of the terrible reputation of the third floor. In fact, if it hadn't been for all of the unforeseen expenses of Dan's hospitalization, she probably would have turned down the promotion and pay raise. So here she was, on the infamous third floor. The third person to have the job in the last two years.

The Third Floor

In her first five weeks on the job she had struggled to understand the work and the people. While mildly surprised that she liked many of the people who worked on three, she quickly realized that the third floor deserved its reputation. She had observed Bob, a five-year veteran on the third floor, letting the phone ring seven times before

overhear 우연히 듣다, 엿듣다 **hassled** 골치 아픈 것 **doze** 꾸벅꾸벅 졸다
excuse 변명 **abundant** 많은 **lame** 불충분한 **clue** 단서 **conviction** 확신
journal 일기 **entry** 입구, 참가자 **compliment** 칭찬

• • •

...the excuses were both abundant and lame. '핑계는 수도 없이 많았고 그
모든 것들이 말도 안 되는 것이다' 여기서 lame은 설명, 변명 등이 불확실한
것을 말한다. 재선에 실패하고 임기를 얼마 남기지 않은 대통령이나 국회의원
을 lame-duck이라고 부르는 것도 같은 맥락이다.

She looked down at last night's entry. 문맥상 entry라는 단어는 일기의
'시작 부분'이라고 해석할 수 있다.

30

purposely breaking the connection by unplugging the cord. She had overheard Martha describing how she handled those in the company who "hassled" her to do her processing faster—she put their file under the out-basket "by mistake." Every time Mary Jane went into the break room there was someone dozing at the table.

Most mornings the phones rang unanswered for ten to fifteen minutes after the official start of the day because the staff was still arriving. When questioned, the excuses were both abundant and lame. Everything was slow motion. The "zombie" description of the third floor was definitely deserved. Mary Jane did not have a clue what to do, only the knowledge and conviction that she must do something and do it soon.

The night before, after the kids were asleep, she had tried to work out her situation by writing in her journal. She looked down at last night's entry:

It may have been cold and dreary outside on Friday, but the view from my internal office window made dreary sound like a compliment. There was no energy there. At times I find it hard to believe there are living human beings on three.

baby shower 아기 탄생을 축하하여 아기에게 필요한 물건들을 선물로 가져오는 파티 **cubicle** 개인용 열람석 **oxygen** 산소 **suck** 빨다, 흡수하다 **hardly** 거의~않다 **wonder** 궁금하다 **in store** 저장하여, 준비하여 **back room operation** 밀실작업 .

• • •

It takes a baby shower or a wedding for anyone to come alive. '살아나게 하기 위해서 누군가의 웨딩이나 베이비 샤워가 필요하다'

They seem to be good people, but whatever spark they may have once had, they have lost. '그들은 모두가 선량하게 보이지만, 과거에 한 번이라도 열정을 지니고 있었다 하더라도 이제는 그 모든 것을 잃어버렸음이 분명하다'

whatever~may : 아무리 ~일지라도(=no matter what~may)

Not much here to get excited about, just lots of transactions which need to be processed. '신이 날 만한 일이 많은 것도 아니고 그저 처리해야 할 서류들만 많을 뿐이다'

It takes a baby shower or a wedding for anyone to come alive. They never get excited about anything that's actually happening at work.

I have thirty employees for whom I am responsible and for the most part they do a slow, short day's work for a low day's pay. Many of them have done the same slow say's work in the same way for years and are totally bored. They seem to be good people, but whatever spark they may have once had, they have lost. The culture of the department is such a powerful and depressing force that new people quickly lose their spark as well. When I walk among the cubicles it feels like all the oxygen has been sucked right out of the air. I can hardly breathe.

Last week I discovered four clerks who were still not using the computer system installed here two years ago. They said they liked doing it the old way. I wonder how many other surprises are in store for me.

I suppose many back room operations are like this. Not much here to get excited about, just lots of transactions which need to be processed. But it

convey 알리다, 나르다 crucial 결정적인, 중대한 taken for granted that
~을 당연한 일로 여기다 ailing 병든 cubicle 칸막이, 열람석 ponder 곰곰
이 생각하다, 심사숙고하다 lifetime 평생 adequate 충분한, 적당한 for-
mulate 명확히 말하다, 공식화하다

• • •

as full-time resident '함께 살고 있다'는 뜻의 숙어

doesn't have to be like this. I must find a way to convey how crucial our work is to the company. Our work allows others to serve the company's customers.

Although our work may be a crucial part of the big picture, it happens behind the scenes and is basically taken for granted. It's an invisible part of the company's radar screen if it wasn't so bad. And believe me, it is bad.

It is not a love for this work which brings any of us to this department. I'm not the only person with money problems on this floor. Many of the women and one of the men are also single parents. Jack's ailing father just moved in with him. Bonnie and her husband now have two grandchildren as full-time residents. The big three are why we are here: salary, security, and benefits.

Mary jane pondered the last sentence she had written in her journal. back room operations had always been lifetime positions. The pay was adequate, and the jobs were secure. Looking at the rows of cubicles and desks outside her office, she formulated some questions. "Does

cherish 소중히 하다 **reshape** 모양을 고치다, 다시 만들다 **consolidate** 합병 정리하다, 통합하다 **retirement** 은퇴, 정년퇴직 **pull back into** 돌아오다 **blur** 흐림, 번짐 **put on hold** (전화를)끊지 않고 기다리다 **in a raw** 연속으로

• • •

Do they realize the extent to which market forces are reshaping this industry? '시장의 힘이 산업을 재구성하고 있다는 것을 그들은 어느 정도 깨닫고 있습니까?' which 이하의 문장은 to의 목적절이다.

The call was followed by a sixty-minute blur of "fire fighting." 직역하면 '그 전화 이후에 불 끄는 작업으로 인해 흐림이 60분간 이어졌다' 60분간 전화통에 불이 나는 통에 사무실이 혼란스러웠다는 뜻으로 해석하면 된다.

• • •

Time is money
시간은 돈이다

미국인들에게 시간은 금이다. 이 aphorism(격언, 경구)은 미국인들의 인생관을 잘 보여 준다. 그들의 mind-sets(의식구조)를 잘 보여주는 일화가 하나 있다. 한 미국인 여성이 치과의사와 오후 3시에 검진 예약을 했다. 이 여자는 3시 조금 전에 병원에 도착했지만 치과의사는 4시가 다 되어서야 병원에 도착했다. 검진을 마치고 집에 돌아간 그녀는 자신의 시급을 계산해 의사가 늦은 시간만큼 진찰료에서 공제해버렸다. 물론 그 의사는 크게 화를 냈지만 그도 미국인인지라 그녀의 합리적인 주장을 반박할 수가 없었다.

my staff know that the security they cherish might be just an illusion? Do they realize the extent to which market forces are reshaping this industry? Do they understand that we will all need to change in order for this company to compete in a rapidly consolidating financial services market? Are they aware that if we don't change we will eventually find ourselves looking for other employment?"

She knew the answers. No. No. No. No. her staff members were set in their ways. They had been left alone in the back room far too long. They were just doing their jobs and hoping that retirement would come before change. And what about herself? Was her view that different?

The ringing phone pulled her back into present. The call was followed by a sixty-minute blur of "fire fighting." First, she found out that an important client file was missing and it was rumored to have last been seen on the third floor. Next, someone from another department was so sick and tired of being put on hold she came to the third floor in person and was creating an unpleasant scene. At least there was some energy to work with. Then someone from legal was disconnected three times in a row. And one of the many staff members out ill today had an important

due 만기 extinguish 소멸하다, 끄다 toxic energy dump 유독성 폐기물 더
미 head for 나아가다, 전진하다 sin 잘못 moan 한탄하다, 투덜투덜 말하다
complaint 불평, 불만, stroll 한가로이 거닐다, 산책하다 waterfront 물가
의 땅, 도시의 해안지역 nibble 물어뜯다 gaze at ~을 응시하다 tranquil
고요한, 적막한 Puget Sound 워싱턴 주 북서부, 태평양의 긴 만 distinct 뚜
렷한, 별개의 have a runny nose 코를 흘리다 gasp 숨이 막히다

project due. After the last fire of the morning was extinguished, Mary Jane reached for her lunch and headed for the door.

The Toxic Energy Dump

Mary Jane had begun leaving the building for lunch during the last five weeks. She knew the cafeteria lunch group would be doing what they always did, discussing the sins of the company and moaning about the third floor. It was now too personal and much too depressing to listen to their complaints. She needed some fresh air.

Most of the time she strolled down the hill to eat lunch ay the waterfront. There, while nibbling on a bagel, she would gaze at the water or watch the tourists mill around the little shops. It was a tranquil setting, and Puget Sound provided her some contract with the natural world.

She had only made it two cubicles from her office when she heard the distinct sound of her phone ringing. It could be the day care, she thought. Stacy did have a runny nose this morning. So she raced back to her office, picking up the phone on the fourth ring. "This is Mary Jane Ramirez," she gasped.

oh, boy 놀람을 나타내는 감탄사 **command** 명령하다, 지휘하다 **cut off midsentence** 말을 중간에서 자르다 **SOB** son of bitch의 약자, 미국의 속어 **as far as** ~하는 한 **paternal** 아버지의, 아버지다운 **stay on top** 훤히 알다 **as if** 마치 ~인 것처럼 **all-morning** 오전 내내 **be convinced that** ~을 확신하다 **in order to** ~하기 위해 **corrosive** (정신적으로)좀 먹는, 신랄한 **pull down** 떨어뜨리다, 쇠약하게 하다

• • •

As if she didn't have a clue. '그녀가 아무것도 모르는 것처럼'
We talked about the corrosive effect of a few departments, where the energy and morale are so low that it pulls everyone down. so...that(매우 ~하여 ~하다)구문이 사용된 문장. 해석하면 '우리는 몇몇 부서의 정신을 좀 먹는 영향에 대해 이야기했다, 그 부서는 에너지와 사기가 너무 낮아서 모두를 끌어내리는 곳이다'

40

"Mary Jane, this is Bill."

Oh, boy, what now, she wondered, as she listened to the voice of her new boss. Bill was another reason she had thought twice about taking the job on three. He had a reputation as a real SOB. As far as she could tell, his reputation was deserved. He would issue commands, cut you off midsentence, and he had an annoying habit of asking about the status of projects in a paternal way. "Mary Jane, are you staying on top of the Station project?" As if she didn't have a clue. Mary Jane was the third manager in two years, and she was beginning to understand that it wasn't just the problems with the people on three, it was also Bill.

"I've just come out of an all-morning meeting with the leadership group, and I want to meet with you this afternoon."

"Sure, Bill, is there a problem?"

"The leadership is convinced that we're in for some tough times and in order to survive, we will need the best from everyone. More productivity from the same employees, or we start making changes. We talked about the corrosive effect of a few departments, where the energy and morale are so low that it pulls everyone down."

descend upon 엄습하다 **touchy-feely** (과장된) 스킨십의, 닭살 돋는 **fire up** 격분하다 **single out** 뽑히다, 선발되다 **embarrass** 난처하다 **grill on** 엄하 게 심문하다, 굽다 **up to** ~에 까지 **appropriate** 적당한, 알맞은 **absolutely** 절대적으로

· · ·

If you're not up to it I need to know so I can make the appropriate changes. '당신이 그렇게 할 수 없다면 내가 알아야 한다, 그래야 내가 적당한 변화를 만들 수 있다'
The stuff you do there is not rocket science. '당신이 하는 일에는 로켓 과 학이 필요 없다' 여기서 rocket science라는 표현은 로켓을 만드는 기술처럼 어려운 일이라는 뜻의 관용 표현이다. 따라서 이 문장을 의역하면 '당신이 하 는 일은 어려울 게 없다' 라는 표현이 된다.

· · ·

That's just kid stuff
그건 어린애들이나 하는 거야

stuff는 구체적으로 어떤 물건을 지칭할 수 없는 상황일 경우 종종 쓰이는 편리 한 단어이다. 예를 들어, What's that stuff? It looks like a piece of tire. '저건 뭐죠?, 타이어 조각처럼 보이는데요' 의 문장에서처럼 쓰인다.

A feeling of dread descended upon Mary Jane.

"The boss went to one of those touchy-feely conferences on spirit in the workplace, and he's all fired up. I don't think it's fair to single out the third floor, but he seems to believe the third floor is the biggest problem."

"He singles out the third floor?"

"Not only did he single out third floor, but he had a special name for it. He called it a 'toxic energy dump.' I don't want one of my departments called a toxic energy dump! It's unacceptable! It's embarrassing."

"A toxic energy dump?"

"Yes. And the boss really grilled me on what I'm doing about it. I told him I shared his concern and that I brought you in to solve the problem. He told me he wants to be kept informed of the progress. So, have you solved it yet?"

Had she solved it yet? she only took the job five weeks ago! "Not yet," she said.

"Well, you have to speed things up, Mary Jane. If you're not up to it I need to know so I can make the appropriate changes. The boss is absolutely convinced we all need more energy, passion, and spirit on the job. I'm not sure why the third floor needs passion and energy. The stuff you do there is not rocket science. Personally, I've never

a bunch of 한 무더기의 **butt of joke** 농담거리 **frustration** 좌절 **hard to take** 받아들이기 힘든 **jerk** (속어로)멍청이 **ablaze** 흥분한, 격한 **rather than** ~이기보다 **impulsively** 충동적으로 **whisper** 속삭이다

· · ·

The words toxic energy dump played over and over in her head. '유독성 폐기물 더미라는 말이 몇 번이고 그녀의 머릿속을 맴돌았다'

expected a lot from a bunch of clerks. I guess the third floor has been the butt of jokes for so long that he thinks if we fix it, we solve the problem. What time can you meet?"

"How about two o'clock, Bill?"

"Two-thirty, OK?"

"Sure."

Bill must have heard the frustration in her voice. "Now don't get upset, Mary Jane. You just get to work on this."

He really is hard to take, she thought ad she hung up the phone. Don't get upset! He is my boss, and the problem is real. But what a jerk.

A Change in Routine

Mary Jane's mind was ablaze as she moved toward the elevators a second time. Rather than heading down the hill to the waterfront as usual, she impulsively turned right on First Street, thinking she needed a longer walk. The words toxic energy dump played over and over in her head.

Toxic energy dump! What next? She was walking along First Street when a small voice inside her head whispered, "The toxic energy is what you hate most about the third floor. Something needs to happen."

stroll 산책하다 **pealing** 왁자지껄한 **frugally** 검소하게 **stay away** 멀리하다 **a crowd of** 많은 **cluster around** ~주위에 때를 지어 모이다 **resist** 저항하다 **dwell on** ~을 (곰곰이) 생각하다 **predicament** 곤경 **turn away** 외면하다 **yell out** 소리 지르다 **dozens of** 수십 명의 **hoist** 들어 올리다 **stumble upon** 우연히 발견하다

· · ·

"Good afternoon, yogurt dudes!" dude라는 단어는 흔히 남자들 사이의 친근한 호칭으로 '너석' 정도로 해석할 수 있다. 하지만 성별의 구분 없이 친근하게 상대방을 부르는 호칭으로도 사용된다. 위 문장을 해석하면 '안녕하세요, 요거트를 들고있는 친구들!' 정도가 된다.

Mary Jane's impulsive stroll down First Street took her to a part of town that was new to her. Sounds of pealing laughter caught her attention and she was surprised to see the public market to her left. She had heard about it, but with her tight financial situation and two young children, she usually avoided specialty markets. With her need to live frugally until the medical bills were paid in full, it was just easier to stay away. She had driven through the area but had never been there on foot.

As she turned and walked down Pike Place, she saw that a large crowd of well-dressed people was clustered around one of the fish markets, and everyone was laughing. At first she felt herself resisting the laughter, dwelling on the seriousness of her predicament. She almost turned away. Then a voice in her head said, "I could use a good laugh," and she moved closer. One of the fish guys yelled out, "Good afternoon, yogurt dudes!" Dozens of well-dressed people then hoisted yogurt cups into the air. My goodness, she thought. What have I stumbled upon?

Pike Place Fish Market 파이크 플레이스 어시장　**play a trick on** ~에 속임수를 쓰다　**distinctive** 특유의, 구별되는　**apron** 앞치마　**in unison** (음악 등을)일제히　**one-handed** 한 손만 사용하는　**applaud** 박수치다, 칭찬하다 **remarkable** 주목할 만한, 두드러진　**slightly** 약간　**thin** 얇은　**juggle** ~로 곡예를 하다　**AARP**(American Association of Retired Persons)미국퇴직자협회 **uncontrollably** 통제할 수 없게　**spectacle** 장관

· · ·

A slightly older fish guy with thinning gray hair was walking around shouting, "Questions, questions, answers to any questions about fish!" '좀 나이가 들어 보이는 머리가 희끗희끗한 상인은 주위를 걸어 다니며 외치고 있었다, "질문 받아요, 질문 받아요, 생선에 관한 질문은 무엇이든 대답해 드립니다."'

48

The world famous Pike Place Fish market

Was that a fish flying through the air? She wondered if her eyes were playing tricks on her; then it happened again. One of the worker—they were distinctive in their white aprons and black rubber boots—picked up a large fish, threw it twenty feet to the raised counter, and shouted, "One salmon flying away to Minnesota." Then all the other workers repeated in unison, "One salmon flying away Minnesota." The guy behind the counter made an unbelievable one-handed catch, then bowed his head to the people applauding his skill. The energy was remarkable.

To her right, another worker was playfully teasing a small boy by making a large fish move its mouth as if it were talking. A slightly older fish guy with thinning gray hair was walking around shouting, "Questions, questions, answers to any questions about fish!" A young worker at the cash register was juggling crabs. Two card-carrying members of AARP were laughing uncontrollably as their fish guy salesman carried on a conversation with the fish they had chosen, The place was wild. She could feel herself relax as she enjoyed the spectacle.

She looked at the people holding the yogurt cups in the

curiosity 호기심 **walk over** (길 등을)건너다 **intently** 골똘히 **stammer** 말을 더듬다 **tease** 괴롭히다, 집적거리다

· · ·

Do they really buy fish at lunch or do they just come to watch the action? '이들이 점심시간에 설마 생선을 사러 온 걸까? 아니면 생동감 넘치는 이곳의 모습을 구경하러 온 것일까?'

Off to her right one of the fish guys, looking lost, was shouting... off to 는 '~로부터 거리가 있는'이란 뜻으로 해석하면 '그녀의 오른쪽에서 좀 떨어진 곳에 한 생선 상인(길을 잃은 듯한)이 외치고 있었다'

· · ·

What brings you here?

여기는 무슨 일로 오셨나요?

What are you doing?의 공손한 표현이다. 상황에 따라서는 상대방의 방문을 의아하게 생각할 때의 질문(당신이 여기 어쩐 일이지요?)이 될 수도 있다.

50

air and thought, Office workers. Do they really buy fish at lunch or do they just come to watch the action?

Mary Jane was unaware that one of the fish guys had noticed her in the crowd. There was something about her curiosity and seriousness which caused him to walk over.

"What's the matter? Don't you have any yogurt?" She looked around and saw a handsome young man with long curly black hair. He was looking at her intently a big smile on his face.

"I have yogurt in the bag," she stammered as she gestured to her brown bag, "but I'm not sure what is happening."

"Have you been here before?"

"No, I usually go down to the waterfront for lunch."

"I can understand that—it's peaceful by the water. Not very peaceful here, that's for sure. So what brings you here today?"

Off to her right one of the fish guys, looking lost, was shouting, "Who wants to buy a fish?" Another was teasing a young woman. A crab sailed over Mary Jane's head. "Six crabs flying away to Montana," someone shouted. "Six crabs flying away to Montana," they all repeated. A fish guy wearing a wool cap was dancing behind the cash

madhouse 소란한 곳 **distract** 흐트러뜨리다 **flinch** 주춤하다 **smack** 찰싹 치다 **identify** 확인하다, 식별하다 **crappy** 엉터리인, 터무니없는 **hesitation** 망설임

• • •

the rides at the state fair state fair는 미국의 각 주(州)마다 열리는 축제를 말한다. 그리고 ride는 탈 것이라는 뜻이다. 따라서 축제에서 탈 것은 놀이기구를 의미한다. 해석하면 '지역 축제의 놀이기구'
I'm spoiled for life. spoil은 '망치다'라는 뜻 외에도 '갈망하다'라는 뜻이 있다. 따라서 이 문장을 해석하면 '간절히 원한다' 정도가 된다.

register. It was a controlled madhouse all around her, like the rides at the state fair, only better. But the fish guy at her side didn't seem at all distracted. He was pleasantly and patiently waiting for her response. My goodness, she thought. He actually seems interested in my answer. But I'm not going to tell a total stranger about my troubles at work. Then she did just that.

His name was Lonnie, and he listened attentively to her description of the third floor. He didn't flinch when one of the flying fish hit a rope and smacked the ground right beside them. He listened closely as she described the many employee problems she had identified. When she finished telling her story, she looked at Lonnie and asked, "So what do you think about my toxic energy dump?"

"That's quite a story. I've worked in some pretty dreary places myself. In fact this place used to be pretty crappy. What do you notice about the market now?"

"The noise, the action, the energy," she said, without a moment's hesitation.

"And how do you like all this energy?"

"I love it," she replied. "I really love it!"

"Me too, I'm spoiled for life. I don't think I could work in a typical market after experiencing this. As I mentioned,

apply 적용하다   **worthwhile** ~할 보람이 있는   **for sure** 확실히, 틀림없이
mess 엉망

• • •

Who knows, you might get some ideas. '누가 알겠어요, 당신이 여기서 아
이디어를 좀 얻을 수 있을지'

the market didn't start this way. It, too, was an energy dump for many years. Then we decided to change things—and this is the result. Would energy like this make a difference with your group?"

"It sure would. It's what we need at the dump," she said, smiling.

"I'd be happy to describe what I think makes this fish market different. Who knows, you might get some ideas."

"But, but we don't have anything to throw! We have boring work to do. Most of us..."

"Slow down. It's not just about throwing fish. Of course your business is different, and it sounds like you have a serious challenge facing you. I'd like to help. What if you could find your own way to apply some of the lessons we learned while becoming the world famous Pike Place Fish market? Wouldn't the possibility of an energized department make it worthwhile for you to learn those lessons?"

"Yes. For sure! But why would you do this for me?"

"Being a part of this little fish market community and experiencing what you see here has made a big difference in my life. I won't bore you with the personal details, but my life was a real mess when I took this job. Working here

sappy 감상적인 **obligation** 의무 **seek out** 찾아내다 **demonstrate** 입증하다 **twang** 콧소리 **fair enough!** (제안에 대하여)좋아 **have no doubt** 의심하지 않다, 확신하다 **glance** 흘긋 봄

· · ·

A chorus echoed. '일제히 외치는 소리가 메아리쳤다'
She had no doubt her arrivals and departures were being clocked by her staff. '그녀는 그녀의 도착과 출발시간이 그녀의 직원들에 의해 기록된다고 확신했다'

has literally saved my life. It may sound a little sappy, but I believe I have an obligation to seek out and find ways to demonstrate my gratitude for this life I enjoy. You made that easy for me by telling me about your problem. I really believe you can find some of your answers here. We've created a lot of great energy." As he said the word energy, a crab sailed by and someone shouted with a Texas twang, "Five crabs flying away to Wisconsin." A chorus echoed, "Five crabs flying away to Wisconsin."

"Fair enough," she answered, laughing out loud. "If the fish market has anything, it has energy. It's a deal." She looked at her watch and realized she would have to walk fast in order to get back to work within the lunch hour. She had no doubt her arrivals and departures were being clocked by her staff.

Lonnie caught her glance and said, "Hey, why don't you come back for your lunch break tomorrow — and bring two yogurts."

He turned and immediately began helping a young man in Vikings jacket understand the difference between a Copper River salmon and King salmon.

emerge 나타나다 ramp 경사로, 진입로 concession 매점 glass-enclosed 유리로 둘러싸인 harbor 항구 fishmonger 생선장수 appeal 호소하다, 애원하다 typical 전형적인 impressive 인상적인 tedious 지루한, 지겨운 mundane 평범한, 세속적인 repetitious 자꾸 되풀이하는, 지루한

• • •

he immediately emerged from the crowd and directed her down a ramp past the T-shirt concession. '그는 군중 속에서 즉시 나타났고 그녀에게 티셔츠 매점 지나서 있는 경사로를 가르켰다'

Return Visit

At lunchtime on Tuesday she walked quickly down First Street to the market. Lonnie must have been watching for her; he immediately emerged from the crowd and directed her down a ramp past the T-shirt concession.

"There are some tables at the end of the hall," he said, and led the way to a small glass-enclosed room with a great view of the harbor and Puget Sound. Lonnie ate a bagel and the yogurt Mary Jane brought him while she ate her yogurt and asked about the workings of a fish market. Fishmongering really didn't sound very appealing after Lonnie told her about a typical day; this made the attitude of the workers at the Pike Place Fish market all the more impressive.

"It would seem that your work and my work have more in common than I thought," she said, after Lonnie described the tedious tasks that needed to be conducted each day.

Lonnie looked up, "Really?"

"Yes, most of the work my staff does can be mundane and repetitious, to say the least. It's important work, however. We never see a customer, but if we make a

fascinate 매혹하다, 주의를 끌다 **dull** 단조롭고 지루한, 따분한 **be performed with** ~로 수행되다

· · ·

...it get old fast. '금방 지루해진다'
I was bored to tears. '나는 눈물이 날 정도로 지루했다'

mistake, the customer is upset and we receive a lot of criticism. If we do our work well, no one notices. In general, the work is boring. You've taken boring work and made the way you do the work interesting. I find that fascinating."

"Have you ever considered the fact that any work can be boring to the person who has to do it? Some of the yogurt dudes travel all over the world for business. It sounds pretty exciting to me, but they tell me it gets old fast. I guess given the right conditions, any job can be dull."

"I agree with what you said. When I was a teenager I had a chance to do a job many teenage girls often dream about: I received a modeling contract. But by the end of the first month I was bored to tears. It was almost all just standing around, waiting. Or take newscasters. I've since learned that many do nothing other than read other people's text. That sounds boring, also — at least to me."

"OK. If we agree that any job can be boring, can we agree that any job can be performed with energy and enthusiasm?"

"I'm not sure. Can you give me an example?"

"That's easy. Walk around the market and look at the

phrase 어구(語句) **pull out** 잡아당기다, 꺼내다 **even if** 비록~일지라도

$$\cdots$$

They don't get it. '그들은 이해하지 못 한다'
We can choose the attitude we bring to our work. '일에 대한 우리의 자세는 우리가 선택할 수 있다'

other fish shops. They don't get it. They are, what was the phrase you used... toxic energy dump. The way they approach their work is really good for our business. I've told you the Pike Place Fish market used to be like them. Then we discovered an amazing thing. There is always a choice about the way you do your work, even if there is not a choice about the work itself. That was the biggest lesson we learned in building the world famous Pike Place Fish market. We can choose attitude we bring to our work."

Choose Your Attitude

Mary Jane pulled out a notepad and began writing:

**There is always a choice about
the way you do your work,
even if there is not
a choice about the work itself.**

Then she thought about the words she had just written, and asked, "Why wouldn't you have choice about the

work itself 일 그 자체 **factor** 요인, 원인 **a great deal of** 대단한 **dispense** 베풀다, 분배하다 **infectious** 전염성의 **likewise** 마찬가지로 **buddy** 동료, 친구 **moody** 침울한, 시무룩한 **grouchy** 지르퉁한, 성난 **irritate** 안절부절 못하는, 참지 못하는 **coworker** 동료

• • •

in that sense '그러한 면에서는'

That's what I mean by choice. '선택이라는 말의 의미가 그것이다'

work itself?"

"Good point. You can always quit your job, and so in that sense you have a choice about the work you do. But it might not be a smart thing to do given your responsibilities and other factors. That's what I mean by choice. On the other hand, you always have a choice about the attitude you bring to the job."

Lonnie continued, "Let me tell you about my grandmother. She always brought love and a smile to her work. All of us grandkids wanted to help in the kitchen because washing dishes with Granma was so much fun. In the process a great deal of kitchen wisdom was dispensed. Us Kids were given something truly precious, a caring adult.

"I realize now that my grandmother didn't love dishwashing. She brought love to dishwashing, and her spirit was infectious

"Likewise, my buddies and I realized that each day when we come to the fish market we bring an attitude. We can bring a grouchy attitude and irritate our coworkers and customers. Or we can bring a sunny, playful, cheerful attitude and have a great day. We can choose the kind of day we will have. We spent a lot of time talking about this

as long as ~하는 한 ordinary 평범한, 보통의 sloppy 질퍽한 determine 결정하다, 결심하다 victim 희생자, 피해자 out of control 통제되지 않는 as well 마찬가지로 assume ~라고 여기다

• • •

...we might as well have the best day we can have. might as well은 '~것 이나 다름없다'라는 뜻으로 문장을 해석하면 '우리는 우리가 가질 수 있는 최 고의 날을 가진 것이나 다름없다'

• • •

I used to have a chip in my shoulder.
나는 공격적이었다

'have a chip one's shoulder'는 화를 잘 내고 공격적인 성향을 나타내는 관 용표현이다. 1800년대 미국에서 소년들이 어깨위에 나무 조각을 올려놓고 서 로 싸움을 걸던 것에서 유래되었다고 한다.

choice, and we realized that as long as we are going to be at work, we might as well have the best day we can have. Make sense to you?"

"It sure does."

"In fact, we got so excited about our choices that we also choose to be world famous. A day spent 'being world famous' is a lot more enjoyable than a day spent being ordinary. Do you see what I am saying? Working in a fish market is cold, wet, smelly, sloppy, difficult work. But we have a choice about our attitude while we are doing that work."

"Yes, I think I get it. You choose the attitude you bring to work each day. That choice determines the way you are at work. As long as you are here, why not choose to be world famous rather than ordinary? It seems so simple."

"Simple to understand, but more difficult to do. We didn't create this place overnight; it took almost a year. I was a hard case myself—you might say I used to have a chip on my shoulder. My personal life was kind of out of control as well. I really never thought much about it, just assumed I knew how life worked. Life was tough, and I responded in kind—I was tough. Then when we decided to create a different kind of fish market, I resisted the

notion 관념, 생각 **victim** 피해자 **quizzically** 짓궂게 **daydream** 공상 **ingredient** 구성 요소, 성분 **core** 핵심

• • •

I had too much invested in being a victim. '나는 희생자가 되는 데 너무 많은 투자를 해왔다'

We aren't shy, are you? 직역하면 '우리는 부끄럼타지 않아요, 그렇죠?'이 다. 이 문맥상에서는 '(전화번호가 가게 곳곳에 써 붙여진 걸로 봐서)우리는 소극적 인 장사꾼이 아니다'

notion that I could choose how I lived each day. I had too much invested in being a victim. One of the older guys, who also had been through some tough times, took me aside and explained it to me, one monger to another. I did some soul searching and decided I would give it a try. I've become a believer. A person can choose their attitude. I know that because I chose mine."

Mary Jane found herself impressed with what she was hearing and also with the person from whom she was hearing it. She looked up to find Lonnie eyeing her quizzically and realized she had been daydreaming.

"Sorry. I'll give it a try. What else explains your success here?"

"There are four ingredients, but this is the core. Without choosing your attitude the others are a waste of time. So let's stop here and save the other three for later. Take the first ingredient and see what you can do with it back on the third floor. Call me when you're ready to discuss the rest. Do you have our number?"

"It's written everywhere in the shop!"

"Oh yeah. We aren't shy, are we? See you later. And thanks for the yogurt."

even though 비록 ~일지라도 **new age** 뉴에이지(新時代) **tubs** 욕조 **stake** 관심, 내기, 이해관계

· · ·

When in doubt, get more data. '확신이 서지 않으면 더 많은 자료를 확보 하라'
Now the stakes are higher, and the timeline is shorter. '지금은 관심이 더 높아졌고 주어진 시간은 더 짧아졌다'

The Courage to Change

The demands of her job kept Mary Jane on treadmill of activity for the next two days. That was her excuse, anyway. But her thoughts were often on her conversation with Lonnie and the idea of choosing the attitude you bring to work. She realized that even though she agreed with the philosophy of the fish market, there was something holding her back. When in doubt, get more data, she thought.

On Friday, she decided to ask Bill about the conference his boss had attended the one about spirit in the workplace. It might be wise to learn more about his experience. That afternoon, she called Bill.

"Bill, how can I get up to speed on the spirit in the workplace conference the big guy attended?"

"What do you want to do that for? It was one of those 'new age' deals. They probably spent most of their in hot tubs. Why do you want to waste your time on that?"

Mary Jane felt herself getting angry. She took a deep breath. "Look, Bill, when I took this job we both knew there was a lot to do. Now the stakes are higher, and the timeline is shorter. You are in this as deep as I am. Are you

evenly 평등하게, 공평하게 confrontational 대립되는, 모순되는 work up
흥분하다, 발전시키다 fill in ~에게 알리다 come by 들르다 commute 통
근하다 bumper to bumper 교통 정체 mull over 곰곰이 생각하다 speak
up 거리낌없이 말하다 courageous 용기 있는 consciousness 의식, 자각
overwhelm 압도하다, 당황하게 하다 resonant 낭랑한 mesmerize 매혹시
키다, 감화시키다

• • •

I'll come by and pick it up. '곧 가지러 가겠다'

...she finally started putting the pieces together at the edge of her
consciousness. '그녀는 마침내 의식의 가장자리에 있는 조각들을 맞추기 시
작했다'

going to help me or give me a hard time?"

I can't believe I said that, she thought. But it sure felt good!

Bill responded evenly; this confrontational approach actually seemed to make him more comfortable. "OK, OK. Don't get all worked up. I have an audio tape from the conference on my desk that I'm supposed to listen to. I just haven't had time. You take it and fill me in?"

"Sure, Bill. I'll come by and pick it up."

A Memorable Commute

The commute to Bellevue was bumper to bumper, but Mary Jane didn't notice. She was mulling over her situation. When did I lose my confidence? she wondered to herself. Speaking up to Bill is the first courageous thing I have done in a long time. Two years to be exact, she realized, as she finally started putting the pieces together at the edge of her consciousness. Too much to think about. Felling overwhelmed, she put Bill's tape into the cassette player.

From the car stereo speakers came a deep, resonant voice that was mesmerizing. The tape was a recording of

verse 운문 **cope with** 대처하다, 극복하다 **recite** 암송하다, 낭송하다 **flexibility** 유연성, 융통성 **wholeheartedness** 전심전력, 진심 **crack** 조금 열린 틈 **corporate** 법인의, 회사의 **upholstery** 가구류, 실내장식품 **breathe out** 숨을 내쉬다

• • •

Phrases jumped out at her. 시의 구절들이 그녀를 사로잡았다는 뜻
...but because sixty percent of us goes into that place, and rest of us stays in the car all day and must breathe out there. '우리 자신의 60%만 회사에 들여보내고 나머지 40%는 하루 종일 차에 남아 숨 쉬어야 하기 때문이다'

74

verse from a poet who took his poetry to the workplace, believing the language of poetry could help us cope with the issues of the day. His name was David Whyte. He would talk a while and then recite a poem. His poems and stories washed over her. Phrases jumped out at her.

The needs of the organization and our needs as workers are the same. Creativity, passion, flexibility, whole-heartedness...

Yes, she thought.

We crack the windows of our cars in the corporate parking lot in the summer, not to save the upholstery from the heat, but because only sixty percent of us goes into that place, and the rest of us stays in the car all day and must breathe out there. What would it be like to take our whole self to work?

Who is this guy? Then without warning, she filled with emotion as she heard David Whyte recite his poem Faith. He introduced it to his audience by saying he wrote it at a time when he had very little faith himself:

fade (빛깔이)바래다, (소리가)사라지다, (꽃이)시들다, (기력이)쇠퇴하다 **curve**
곡선 **sliver** 가느다랗게 하다 **slender** 가느다란, 미덥지 않은 **barely** 간신히,
겨우

· · ·

faithful even as it fades from fullness '그 충만함을 서서히 잃어가더라도
그 믿음은 여전히 남아 있다'
sliver of light before the final darkness '마지막 어둠 전의 빛 한 조각'

Faith

by David Whyte

I want to write about faith
about the way the moon rises
over cold snow, night after night

faithful even as it fades from fullness
slowly becoming that last curving and impossible
sliver of light before the final darkness
but I have no faith myself
I refuse to give it the smallest entry

Let this then, my small poem,
like a new moon, slender and barely open,
be the first prayer that opens me to faith

insight 통찰력 **risky** 위험한, 모험적인 **survivor** 생존자, 역경에 지지 않는 사람

• • •

the dump-Carter movement 과거 민주당 내의 카터 대통령 퇴진공작에서도 dump라는 단어가 사용되었다. Their anxiety diminished with distance from Washington, where endangered Democratic congressmen first fomented the dump-Carter movement. '워싱턴으로부터 멀어짐에 따라 민주당원들의 걱정은 사라졌다. 자기의 정치 생명에 위험을 느낀 민주당 의원들이 처음 카터 퇴진공작을 시작한 것은 워싱턴에서의 일이었다.'

So this is what is meant by the statement, "When the student is ready the teacher appear." The poem had created a moment of insight, and Mary Jane finally saw what was holding her back. With Dan's sudden death and the pressures of being a responsible single mom, she had lost faith in her ability to survive in the world. She was afraid that if she took a risk and failed, she would not be able to support herself and her children.

Leading a change at work would be risky. She could fail and lose her job. That was a distinct possibility. Then she thought about the risk of not changing. If we don't change, we could all lose our jobs. Not only that: I don't want to work in a place with no energy or life. I know what it will do to me over time, and the picture is nor pretty. What kind of a mother would I be if let that happen? What example would I set? If I launch the change process on Monday, the first step must be for me to choose my attitude. I choose faith. I must trust that whatever happens I will be all right.

I'm a survivor; I've proven that. I will be all right, whatever happens. It's time to clean up the toxic energy dump. Not just because it would be good for business— although I believe it will be great for business. And not

external 외부의 **renew** 새롭게 하다 **tackle** 논쟁하다 **necessarily** 반드시,
물론 **prison** 감옥 **metaphor** 은유 **encounter** 마주치다, 맞닥뜨리다 **precious** 귀중한 **recognizable** 인식할 수 있는, 알아볼 수 있는

· · ·

The prison metaphor had a familiar ring. '감옥 은유와 비슷한 울림을 가
졌다' 그녀가 과거에 경험했던 어떤 것(생각)과 비슷하다는 뜻으로 이해할 수
있다.

**Life is too precious to spend any time at all, much less half of my
saving hours, in a toxic energy dump.** '유독성 폐기물 더미에서 내 귀중한
시간의 절반을 보내기엔 내 인생은 너무 소중합니다' 여기서 saving은 '귀중
한' 정도로 번역하면 좋다.

· · ·

She really comes on hard

그 여자는 정말 진하게 유혹하는군.

미국 영어에서는 come on이 명사형으로 쓰이면 보통 salesman의 능수능란한
판매술을 나타낸다. 하지만 동사형으로 쓰이면 seduce(유혹하다)의 뜻이 된다.

just because I have been challenged to solve the problem—that is an important reason, but it's an external issue. The compelling reason to move ahead comes from my inside. I need to renew my faith in myself, tacking this problem will help me do just that.

She remembered some lines from the tape: "I don't believe that companies are necessarily prisons, but sometimes we make prison of them by the way we choose to work there. I have created a prison and the walls are my own lack of faith in myself."

The prison metaphor had a familiar ring—she was sure she had encountered it before in a seminar she had attended. As soon as she arrived at the daycare, she parked her car, took out her journal, and wrote:

Life is too precious to spend any time at all, much less half of my walking hours, in a toxic energy dump. I don't want live like that, and I am sure my associates will feel the same way once they have a recognizable choice.

The culture in my department has been the way it is for a long time. In order to change the culture, I will need to take personal risks with no

assurance 보장 **bless** 축복 **timely** 시기적절한 **figure** 모습, 계산
sweetheart 애인, 여보, 당신, 애착 가는 물건 혹은 사람을 부르는 호칭
exhaled 숨을 내쉬다

• • •

**Somewhere in my files is material which contains a message that could
be timely.** '내 파일 중 어딘가에 시기적절한 내용을 담은 자료가 있다'

assurance of success. This could be a blessing. Recent events have shaken my faith in myself and taking the necessary risks could help me renew my faith. The fact is that the risk of doing nothing is probably greater than the risk of acting.

Somewhere in my files is material which contains a message that could be timely. I need to find that message because I need all the help I can get.

With that she got out of the car and went in to pick up her daughter.

"Mommy, Mommy. Your eyes are wet. Have you been crying? What's wrong, Mommy?"

"Yes, sweetheart, I've been crying, but it was good crying. How was your day?"

"I made a picture of our family, do you want to see it?"

"I sure do." She looked down and saw the four figures her daughter had drawn, looking back at her. "Oh boy," she exhaled. Another test of faith.

"Get your things honey; we have to go pick up Brad."

sitter 베이비시터(유모) **inspirational** 영감의, 고무적인 **sip** 한 모금 **grab** 부여잡다, 움켜쥐다 **tatter** 찢어진 조각, 넝마 **abundance** 풍부

Sunday Afternoon

Sunday afternoon was Mom's time. Mary Jane arranged to have a sitter for at least two hours every Sunday. It was a little reward she gave herself, one which always left her refreshed and ready for the challenges of work and family. She used the time to read inspirational material or a good novel, go for a bike ride, or just sip coffee and relax. Seattle was full of coffee shops and there was a great spot three blocks away. She grabbed some books and headed out. Her favorite table in a private corner of the shop was waiting for her.

"Grande skinny latte please." She sat down with her latte and decided to start with inspirational reading. She pulled out her tattered copy of Sarah Ban Breathnach's Simple abundance, a book which contains a reading for every day of the year, and turned to February 8. Key words seemed to jump off the page:

Most of us are uncomfortable thinking of ourselves as artists... But each of us is an artist... With every choice, every day, you are creating a unique work of art. Something that only you can do... The reason you were

indelible 지울 수 없는, (오점 등이)잊혀지지 않는 **authenticity** 확실성, 신뢰성 **urge** 충동, 자극 **sonnet** 14행 시(詩) **startling** 놀라운 **generous** 관대한, 마음이 넓은 **page by page** 한 쪽씩

• • •

What is more, you will discover that your life is all it was meant to be.
'게다가, 당신은 당신의 삶이 모두 의도한 대로 되는 것을 발견할 것이다'

born was to leave your own indelible mark on the world. This is your authenticity... Respect your creative urges... step out in faith... you will discover your choices are as authentic as you are. What is more, you will discover that your life is all it was meant to be: a joyous sonnet of thanksgiving.

She had planned on thinking a little bit about work, and the words about choice and faith took her back to the fish market. Those guys are artists, she thought, and they must choose to create each day. And she had a startling thought: I can be an artist, too.

Then, she took out a file from a leadership seminar she had attended. This was where she first heard prison being used as a metaphor for work. Inside was a faded photocopy of a speech written by John Gardner. She recalled that Gardner encouraged people to reproduce his papers, a generous gesture, she thought. He must have said something powerful if I remember him after all this time. She searched through the speech, page by page.

vital 생기 있는 **vague** 흐릿한, 멍청한 **imply** 포함하다, 내포하다 **compassionate** 인정 많은, 동정심 있는 **assess** 평가하다, 사정하다 **inflict** 주다, (상처 등을) 입히다 **wound** 상처 **self-esteem** 자존심, 자부심

• • •

There is the puzzle of why some men and woman go to seed, while others remain vital to the very end of their days. '왜 어떤 사람들은 쇠퇴하는데 반해 다른 사람들은 삶의 마지막까지 생기 있는지 의문이다' 여기서 'go to seed'를 직역하면 '씨를 뿌리다' 정도가 된다. 어떤 식물이 씨를 뿌리는 시기를 삶의 마지막 단계에 비유한 관용표현이다. 따라서 여기서는 '쇠퇴하다', '초라해지다'라는 뜻으로 해석하면 된다.

The Writing of John Gardner

The passage began:

There is the puzzle of why some men and women go to seed, while others remain vital to the very end of their days. Going to seed may be too vague an expression. Perhaps I should say that many people, somewhere along the line, stop learning and growing.

Mary Jane looked up as she thought, That fits my group. And it fits the old me, as well. She smiled at the decision implied by "the old me." She went back to the passage:

One must be compassionate in assessing the reasons. Perhaps life just presented them with tougher problems than they could solve. Perhaps something inflicted a major wound to their self-confidence or their self-esteem... Or maybe they just ran so hard for so long that they forgot what they were running for.
I'm talking about people who, no matter how busy they may seem, have stopped learning ad growing. I don't

deride 비웃다, 조소하다 **keep on doing** 계속하다 **stale** 싱싱하지 못한, 한
물간 **be convinced that** ~을 확신하다 **countervail** 대항하다, 무효로 만들
다 **measure** 측정, 도구 **wind up** (태엽을) 감다 **tap** 가볍게 두드리다
exploit 개척하다, 개발하다

deride that. Life is hard. Sometimes just to keep on keeping on is an act of courage...

We have to face the fact that most men and women out there in the world of work are more stale than they know, more bored than they would care to admit...

A famous French writer said, "There are people whose clocks stop at a certain point in their lives." I've watched a lot of people move through life. As Yogi Berra says, "You can observe a lot by watching." I am convinced that most people enjoy learning and growing, at ant time in their life. If we are aware of the danger of going to seed we can take countervailing measures. If your clock is unwound you can wind it up again.

There is something I know about you that you may not even know about yourself. You have within you more resources of energy than have ever been tapped, more talent than has ever been exploited, more strength than has ever been tested, and more to give than you have ever given.

No wonder I remember John Gardner. I have a lot of clocks to wind up, but first I need to wind up my own,

look over 대충 훑어보다　**take action** 조치를 취하다, 행동을 취하다　**might as well** 차라리~하는 편이 낫다　**in every sense of the word** 모든 의미에서 **pang** 격통, 마음의 고통

· · ·

No wonder I remember John Gardner. '내가 존 가드너를 기억하는 것은 놀랄 만한 일이 아니다'
There is no safe harbor. '안전한 항구는 없다'는 뜻으로 여기서는 '안전한 일이란 없다'라고 이해하면 된다.

she thought.

For the next hour Mary Jane wrote in her journal and was pleased to note that she had become quite peaceful. As she prepared to return home, she looked over what she had written and circled the section that would be her guide on Monday morning.

> *Solving the problem of the toxic energy dump will require me to become a leader in every sense of the word. I will need to risk the possibility of failure. There is no safe harbor. But to take no action is to fail for sure. I might as well get started. My first step is to choose my attitude. I choose confidence, trust, and faith. I will wind up my clock and get ready to enjoy learning and growing as I work to apply the lessons from the fish market to my toxic energy dump.*

Monday Morning

At 5:30 A.M. she felt some pangs of guilt as she sat outside her daughter's daycare center, waiting for the doors to open. On rare days like this, Brad would also stay at the

pipe up 갑자기 소리 높여 말하다　**personalize** 개인화하다

daycare until a bus took him to school. She looked over at the sleepy-eyed kids and said, "I won't get you out of bed so early very often kids, bet today I need to get to the office to prepare for a really important project."

Brad rubbed his eyes and said, "That's all right, Mom." Then Stacy piped up, "Yeah, it's fun to get here first. We get first pick of video games!"

When the doors opened, Mary Jane signed them in and gave them each a big hug. When she looked back they were already busy.

It was an easy commute; by 5:55, she was at her desk with a steaming cup of coffee and a pad. She took out a pen and wrote in large letters:

CHOOSE YOUR ATTITUDE

Steps:
- Call a meeting and speak from the heart.
- Find a message that communicates the notion of choosing your attitude in a way that everyone will understand and personalize.
- Provide motivation.

persist 주장하다, 고집하다 **two shifts** 2교대 **assemble** 모이다, 집합하다
universal 보편적인, 우주의 **enthusiastic** 열광적인 **recruitment** 채용

· · ·

Here goes everything. 'Everything goes here'를 강조하기 위한 문장으로
'모든 것이 여기서 진행된다' 는 뜻이다.

- Persist with faith.

Now the tough part. What do I say to my staff here on three? And she began writing down her thoughts.

On Monday mornings the staff met in two shifts; one group covered the phones while the other met with her in the conference room-then they switched. As the first group assembled, she listened to the discussions of family activity and universal complaints about Monday morning. These are good people, she thought; she felt her heart beating faster as they quieted and turned their attention to her. Here goes everything.

Mary Jane's Presentation

"Today we have a serious issue to discuss. A couple of weeks ago the group vice president went to a conference and returned convinced that First Guarantee needs to become a place that is more energetic and enthusiastic. He is convinced that energy and enthusiasm are the keys to productivity, successful recruitment, long-term retention,

host 진행자, 운영자 **consolidate** 합병정리하다, 통합하다 **refer to** ~로 강조하다 **accusation** 비난 **go away** 사라지다 **VP** vice president(부사장, 중역) **pit** 구덩이

• • •

Heck, many of us hate coming here. '젠장, 우리 중의 대다수도 여기오길 싫어해요.' heck은 hell(지옥)의 완곡한 표현으로, 강한 감정을 표현할 때 문장 중에 끼워서 사용하는 구어적 표현이다. 예를 들어 'What do you want?'라는 문장에 heck을 사용해 What the heck do you want? '도대체 뭘 원하는 거야?'처럼 좀더 강한 뉘앙스로 만들 수 있다.

great customer service, and a host of other qualities that we need in order to compete in our changing and consolidating business. He called a meeting of the leadership group—and at that meeting he referred to the third floor as a 'toxic energy dump.' That's right, he called our floor a toxic energy dump and said it needed to be cleaned."

Mary Jane looked at the startled expressions. A comment came quickly from Adam, a long-term employee: "I'd like to see them do this work. It's the most boring work on earth."

Then one of the least energetic employees said, "What difference dose it make if there is energy here? We get the work done, don't we?"

No one challenged the accusation that their energy was toxic.

Mary Jane continued, "I want you to know that this issue is not going away. Oh, the group VP may lose interest, and Bill might forget abut it with, but I will not. You see, I am in full agreement. We are a toxic energy dump. Other parts of the company hate dealing with us. They also call us 'the pit.' They joke about us at lunch. They laugh about us in the halls. And they are right. Heck, many if us hate coming here, and even we call this a pit.

stun 대경실색케 하다 **startle** 깜짝 놀라게 하다 **precious** 귀중한

• • •

Here is the bottom line. '결론은 이것이다' 모든 글의 마지막에 결론이 나오듯이 'bottom line'은 '결론'이란 뜻의 관용표현이다.

• • •

We are closed for the day.
오늘 일은 끝났습니다.

은행 같은 곳에 좀 늦게 전화를 걸면 전화 받은 사람이 'We are closed for the day'라고 말하는 경우가 있다. 이 말은 "오늘 일은 끝내고 문을 닫았습니다"라는 뜻이다. 여기서 the day는 today를 뜻하므로 closed for the day는 "오늘 일은 끝냈다"라는 말이 된다.

또 어떤 회사에 전화해 누군가를 바꿔 달라고 했을 때 'He is gone for the day'라고 말한다면 '오늘 일을 끝내고 퇴근했다'는 뜻이다.

I think we can and should change that; I want you to know why."

The startled expressions were now replaced with truly stunned expressions. The silence was complete.

"You all know my story. How Dan and I came to town with our hopes, dreams, and two small children. How Dan's sudden death left me alone. How Dan's insurance didn't cover many of the big expenses. How I found myself in a difficult financial position.

"What you may not know is how all this affected me. Some of you are single moms and dads and know what I am talking about. I needed this jobs, and I had lost my confidence. I went with the flow, never doing anything that could threaten my security. It seems funny that my security is now threatened and it may be because I went with the flow. Well, those days are over.

"Here is the bottom line. I still need this job, but I don't want to spend the rest of my working life in a toxic energy dump. Dan's lesson had been lost on me until now. Life is too precious just to be passing through to retirement. We simply spend too much time at work to allow it to be wasted. I think we can make this a better place to work.

consultant 조언가, 고문 **eventually** 결국 **nod** 끄덕이다 **cut off** 끼어들다
honk 경적을 울리다 **suburb** 교외, 시외

• • •

Life is too precious just to be passing through to retirement. 'to pass through' 라고 할 수도 있지만 지금도 인생을 그냥 흘려 보내고 있기 때문에 진행형을 사용했다.

a tough part of town '도시의 위험한 지역' 정도로 해석하면 된다.

"Now the good news. I know a consultant who works for a world famous organization and is an expert on energy. You will meet him eventually. Today I am going to convey his first bit of advice: We choose our attitude."

Mary Jane continued by discussing the concept of choosing your attitude. Then she asked if there were any questions.

Steve raised his hand. When Mary Jane nodded to him, he said, "Suppose I'm driving my car and some idiot cuts me off in traffic. That causes me to get upset and I may honk or even make a gesture, if you know what I mean. What's with the choice thing? I didn't do it; it was done to me. I didn't have a choice."

"Let me ask you something, Steve. If you were in a tough part of town, would you have used that gesture?"

Steve smiled. "No way! You can get hurt doing that."

"So you can choose your response in a tough part of town, but you have no choice in the suburbs?"

"OK, Mary Jane. OK, I get it."

"You couldn't have asked a better questions, Steve. We can't control the way other people drive, but we can choose how we respond. Here at First Guarantee we don't have a lot to do with selecting the work that needs to be

depend on ～에 달려있다 drain (체력 등이)쇠진하다, 배수하다 embarrass
무안하게 하다, 당황하게 하다 victim 희생자

• • •

"Boy, you really nailed me at the staff meeting." '직원회의에서 당신 정
말 나를 꼼짝 못하게 만들었어요' 여기서 'nail'은 '꼼짝 못하게 만들다'라는
뜻으로 쓰였다.

My life has been a series of reactions lately. '최근의 내 삶은 무기력의 연
속이었다' 'reaction'은 '반작용, 반항, 반응'이라는 뜻으로 주로 쓰이지만 여
기서는 '무기력'이라는 뜻으로 해석하는 것이 좋다.

done, but we can choose how we approach that work. I want all of you to think of ways this is true and see if you can identify things we can do to remind ourselves of our choices. Good luck. Our work life depends on it."

The second staff meeting was much like the first. When she didn't get any questions, she used Steve's question from the first group. It was 10:30 on Monday morning. She was drained from the meetings, but realized it was her first opportunity to choose her attitude. And she did.

The week sped by. She made a point of walking around the office each day and being available to talk about the idea of choosing your attitude. When she saw Steve, he said, "Boy, you really nailed me at the staff meeting."

"I hope I didn't embarrass you."

"Mary Jane, you did me a big favor. My life has been a series of reactions lately. You reminded me that I have important choices to make and that I can make them if I have a little self-control and courage."

"Courage?"

"I am in a bad relationship; I need to do something about it. I can see now that reacting and feeling like a victim is not going to solve the problem. The problem

confront 직면하다, 맞서다 evasive 애매한 be under attack 공격받고 있다
keep at ~에 꾸준히 힘쓰다 down below 저 아래쪽에 frown 얼굴을 찡그
리다 ecstatic 황홀한

needs to be confronted. I'm sorry to be so evasive, but it is rather personal."

"Good luck, Steve, and thanks for trusting me with your story."

"Oh, we all tryst you, Mary Jane. It's just that this work is so boring and all we hear are complaints. We feel like we're always under attack. Keep at it; I'm behind you all the way."

She was pleasantly surprised by the many words of encouragement. While staff members were not sure about the details, most liked the idea of creating a more satisfying work environment.

Then on Friday it happened. She walked off the elevator on the third floor and was confronted with a giant poster. On the top it said: CHOOSE YOUR ATTITUDE, and in the middle were the words: MENU CHOICES FOR THE DAY. Down below the menu were two drawings. One was a smiling face and the other was a frowning face. She was ecstatic. They do get it! she thought to herself and raced to her office to call Lonnie.

After telling him about the menu, she suggested they finish their discussion. Lonnie asked about lunch Monday. Mary Jane said she really didn't want to wait until next

foolishly 어리석게도 **drowsy** 꾸벅꾸벅 조는 **settle on** 결정하다 **wired** 기대로 무장한 **be struck by** ~이 인상적이다 **spot** 발견하다 **neatly** 깔끔하게 **customary** 습관적인

week, so they agreed she should come to the market on Saturday and bring the kids with her.

Saturday at the Fish Market

Saturdays are always busy at the market; Lonnie suggested they come early. Mary Jane foolishly asked what the earliest time was they might arrive. Lonnie said he started work at 5 A.M. They settled on 8.

Brad and Stacy got in the car drowsy, but by the time they had all made the trip into Seattle and found a parking spot, her kids were wired and ready for action. The questions were unending. "Where do they get the fish? Are they big fish? Do they have any sharks? Will there be other kids there?"

As the three walked down Pike Place to the market, Mary Jane was struck by how quiet and calm it was. She immediately spotted Lonnie standing by the fish display. She was impressed with how neatly organized the stand was, with the fish and seafood packed in ice and signs detailing names, prices, and special qualities. One section was empty except for the ice.

"Good morning," said Lonnie with his customary

display 진열 **bewilder** 당황하게 하다 **mammoth cart** 거대한 수레 **hang on** 매달리다

· · ·

Brad was hanging on to the handle with his feet just touching the ground. '브래드는 발이 바닥에 겨우 닿은 채로 손잡이에 매달려 있었다'

smile. "And who are these two fishmongers?"

Mary Jane introduced her children. Lonnie welcomed them and said it was time to get to work. As she was removing her notepad from her purse, he stopped her and said, "No, not that kind of work. I thought you three could help me finish this display."

"Cool," said Brad.

"I couldn't find any boots your size, but I did find three aprons to wear. Here, put these on and we'll start packing fish."

Stacy looked a little bewildered; Mary Jane gave her a quick hug. Lonnie took Brad into the back of the store to visit the fish locker, while Mary Jane kept Stacy entertained with a walk among the displays. In about fifteen minutes, Lonnie and Brad returned pushing a mammoth cart full of fish. To be exact, Lonnie was pushing the cart—Brad was hanging on to the handle with his feet just touching the ground.

PLAY

"Mom! Wow! It rocks back there! There must be a

pretend ~인 척하다 **turn over** 넘겨주다 **subtle** 미묘한, 포착하기 어려운
energy-filled 힘이 가득 찬

million fish. Isn't that right, Lonnie? I got to help, too!" Lonnie gave him a big smile and a nod, but pretended to be all business. "We have to pack these fish so the market can open, little buddy. Ready to give me a hand?"

Brad was having a ball. He would help Lonnie pick up a tuna and Lonnie would pack it in ice, adding to a neat row of fish. The tuna were almost as big as Brad, and Mary Jane was sorry she didn't bring her camera. The way Lonnie worked with Brad was magic. Once in a while Lonnie would trick Brad, pretend the fish bit him, or do something that caused Brad to laugh. When there was room for only two more tuna in the row, Lonnie turned the job over to Brad, but provided some subtle help lifting. If Brad were asked to pick his "action hero" at that moment, he would have chosen Lonnie.

"Now it's time for your mom to get to work. Take out that notebook, Mary Jane, and Brad will give you the second ingredient of an energy-filled workplace."

"Brad?"

"You bet. The second ingredient selected by a bunch of fishmongers who choose their attitude is something that is familiar to any kid. We just forget its importance as we become older and more serious. Brad, tell your mom what

at recess 휴식시간에 pin 꼼짝 못하게 누르다 flash back 과거로 되돌아가다 witness 목격하다 call out 소리쳐 구하다 order 주문 manner 예의 turnover 이직률, 전직률 tedious 지루한 pride 자부심

• • •

You know, not get all uptight, but let things flow. '보다시피, 모든 것을 완벽하게 하는 것이 아니라 그냥 흘러가게 놔두는 거죠' 'you know'은 구어체 표현으로 '보다시피, 알다시피'라는 뜻으로 해석하며 대화 도중 상대방의 호응이나 동의를 구할 때 사용하다.

you do at recess."

Brad looked over the top of the tuna that was pinning him to the edge of the counter and said, "Play."

Mary Jane opened her journal and made a new note: PLAY! Her mind flashed back to the scene at the market she witnessed on that frist day. She had been looking at a playground with adult kids at recess. Throwing fish, kidding with eack other and the customers, calling out orders, repeating the calls. The place had been electric.

"Don't misunderstand," said Lonnie. "This is a real business which is run to make a profit. This business pays a lot of salaries, and we take the business seriously, but we discovered we could be serious about business and still have fun with the way we conducted business. You know, not get all uptight, but let things flow. What many of our customers think of as entertainment is just a bunch of adult kids having a good time, but doing it in a respectful manner.

"And the benefits are many. We sell a lot of fish. We have low turnover. We enjoy work that can be very tedious. We have become great friends, like the players on a winning team. We have a lot of pride in what we do and the way we do it. And we have become world famous.

address ~에게 말을 걸다 **come over** 들르다 **sushi** 초밥 **penny** =cent(1/100 달러) **crook** 구부러지다, 갈고리 **unruly** 흐트러지기 쉬운 **track** 추적하다 **prey** 먹이 **domesticate** 길들이다 **grandfatherly** 할아버지 같은

• • •

All from doing something which Brad does without much thought. '브래드가 별 생각 없이 하는 모든 일처럼'

All from doing something which Brad does without much thought. We know how to play!"

Brad said, "Hey, Mom, why don't you bring the people at work to Lonnie so he can teach them how to play?"

MAKE THEIR DAY

Suddenly someone addressed Mary Jane from the side. "Hey, reporter lady, want to busy a fish?" One of Lonnie's associates had come over and was holding a huge fish head in his hand. "I'll give you a great deal on this one. It's missing a few parts but the price is right." He made the fish's mouth into a smile and said, "I call it smiling sushi. Just a penny." And he looked at her with a crazy, crooked smile.

Lonnie was laughing and, of course, Brad wanted to hold it. Stacy was hiding behind Mom's legs. Mary Jane took out a penny and gave it ti the fish guy they called "Wolf." She didn't need to ask why they called him Wolf. His hair was unruly and his eyes tracked everything as if it were prey. This wolf was clearly domesticated, however, and if such a thing were possible, Wolf had a grandfatherly

beaming 기쁨에 넘친 **bring over** 갖고 오다 **stand out** 눈에 띄다, 뚜렷하게 남아 있다 **slippery** 미끄러운 **memorable** 기억할 만한 **animate** 눈에 띄다 **identify** 일체감을 가지다

· · ·

But she had a ball. '그러나 그녀는 즐거운 한 때를 보냈다' 'have a ball'은 구어적 표현으로 '즐거운 한 때를 보내다'라는 의미를 갖는다.

· · ·

How young are you?

몇 살이세요?

미국인들은 나이가 많고 적음에 별로 개의치 않는다. 스스로 젊다고 느끼면 젊은 것이라고 생각한다. 그래서 그들은 젊음을 늘 소중히 여기고 늙어 가는 것을 존경의 눈으로 바라본다. 그래서 미국인들은 자신을 어떤 특정 연령집단으로 나누는 것을 싫어한다. 그러므로 나이든 미국인에게 'How old are you?' 라고 물으면 기분 나빠할지도 모를 일이다.

air about him. Wolf put the smiling sushi in a bag and gave it to Brad, who was beaming. Shy Stacy piped up for the first time that morning and said she wanted one, too. Wolf brought over two more. Now they all had a smiling sushi.

Lonnie said, "Thanks, Wolf. You just showed us the third ingredient in creating a high-energy, would famous market."

"He did?"

"Think back to the first two times you were here, Mary Jane. What stands out in your mind?"

"I remember a young redheaded woman, about twenty years old. She got up on the platform and tried to catch a fish. Of course she found them a little slippery and missed twice. But she had a ball."

"Why was that so memorable?"

"She was so animated, so alive. And the rest of us in the crowd identified with her. We could imagine ourselves in her place."

"And what do you think Brad will remember about today?"

"Doing big-guy stuff, visiting the cold fish locker, and working with you."

"We call that make their day. We look for as many

engage 약속하다, 보증하다, 관여하다 **apart from** ~와 관계없이 **afterward** 나중에 **a constant flow of positive feelings** 긍정적인 느낌의 지속적인 흐름

· · ·

Let's make some time.

좀 더 빨리 갑시다.

'make some time'은 하나의 숙어로서 'travel at a quicker pace', 'hurry up' 이라는 뜻이다.

ways as we can to create great memories. And we create great memories whenever we make someone's day. The playful way we do our work allows us to find creative ways to engage our customers. That's the key word: engage. We try not to stand apart from our customers but to find ways to respectfully include them in our fun. Respectfully. When we are successful, it makes their day."

Mary Jane opened her journal again and wrote: MAKE THEIR DAY. Her mind filled with thoughts: They engage people and welcome them to join in the fun. Customers like being a part of the show, and memories are created here which will bring smiles and make good stories for a long time afterward. Involving others and working to "make their day" directs attention toward the customer. Great psychology. Focusing your attention on ways to make another person's day provides a constant flow of positive feelings.

"Hello, anyone home?"

Lonnie, Brad, and Stacy were all staring at her. "Sorry, I got to thinking about how powerful an ingredient that is. I hope we can find a way to apply make their day at First Guarantee."

"The market is opening. Let's take the kids for

rapidly 재빠르게 **marvel** 놀라다, 경탄하다 **lighthearted** 근심걱정 없는, 마음 편한 **vigilant** 방심하지 않는, 조심성 있는 **roam** 두리번거리다 **cranky** 까다로운, 변덕스런 **modification** 변형

something to eat; we can finish our discussion there. You kids hungry?"

"Yeah!"

BE PRESENT

They found a table at the cafe across the street and ordered coffee, hot chocolate, and sweet rolls. The market was rapidly filling with people, and Lonnie directed her attention to the way the fish guys interacted with those people. He asked her to watch them in action and told her she would discover the final ingredient if she watched carefully. Her eyes went from one monger to another, marveling at their work. She then turned her attention to those who were between activities. They looked vigilant, eyes roaming for the next opportunity for action.

It was actually a bad experience from the night before that helped her find the answer. She remembered her trip to the store with two cranky kids, both ready for bed. How long did she stand at the counter waiting for a clerk who was talking to another clerk about the modifications he made to his car? It seemed forever as the kids pulled on

impatient 성급한, 참을성 없는 wonder if ~인지 궁금하다 daydream 공
상하다 flash (미소 등을)흘끗 보내다 boyish 소년 같은 grin 싱긋 웃음
focus on 집중하다 be willing to 기꺼이 ~하다 overdo 지나치게 하다, 도
를 넘기다

• • •

It seemed forever as the kids pulled on her dress with impatience. '아
이들이 참을성 없이 그녀의 옷을 잡아 당길 때 그 상황은 영원할 것처럼 보였
다' 여기서 as는 '~할 때' 라는 뜻으로 쓰였다.

They are fully engaged in their work. '그들은 완전히 그들의 일에 관여하
고 있었다'

Be present '현재에 있다'는 뜻으로 '현재에 충실하다'라는 의미로 이해하면
된다.

I'm all ears. '열심히 듣고 있다' 라는 뜻이다. 즉 내가 전부 귀가 될 정도로 열
심히 듣고 있다는 말이다.

her dress with growing impatience. That wouldn't happen here, she thought. These guys are present. They are fully engaged in their work. I wonder if they even daydream? She saked Lonnie if that was the answer.

"You got it. Why am I not surprised?" He flashed his boyish grin. "Look out toxic energy dump, here she comes!" Then Lonnie continued, "I was at the grocery store, waiting my turn at the meat counter. The staff was pleasant and having a good time. The problem was they were having a good time with each other, not me. If they had included me in their fun, it would have been a whole different experience. They had most of it right but were missing the key ingredient. They weren't present and focused on me, the customer. They were internally focused."

She opened her journal and wrote: BE PRESENT. Lonnie was showing his first sign of not being present. She knew why when he said, "I need to get back to work. The guys were more than willing to cover for me, but I don't want to overdo it. There is, however, one piece of advice I would like to offer before I leave."

"I'm all ears."

"Well, I don't mean to tell you how to do your job but I

in a rush to ~하는 데 급급한 나머지　**internalize** 자기 것으로 하다, 내면화
하다　**tuck away** 치우다, 감추다　**briefly** 간단히　**expand on** 자세히 말하다

think it will be important for you to find a way for your staff to discover the Fish Philosophy for themselves. I'm not sure just telling them about the Fish Philosophy will do the trick. Brad had a good idea when he said you should bring them here."

"You and Brad make quite a team. In my rush to solve the problem, I could easily forget that the members of my staff need to have learning experiences of their own, and time to internalize the experience. Thanks so much — for everything. You made our day."

Brad couldn't stop talking on the way home; it was all she could do to be present for him. One somewhat crazy idea found its way into her head. She grinned and tucked it away for Monday.

She told me and then I
discovered it for myself.
– Unknown

Sunday Afternoon

During her private time on Sunday afternoon, Mary Jane opened her journal and briefly expanded on her notes.

come up with ~을 제안하다 **terrific** 굉장한 **explore** 탐구하다, 탐험하다
awareness 자각, 인식 **playground** 놀이터 **atmosphere** 분위기, 대기
inclusion 포함, 함유물 **scan the crowd** 군중을 꼼꼼히 살피다

• • •

Not at all like the boss I had in L.A. who talked to me like I was a tape recorder... '내가 녹음기인 것처럼 나에게 말했던 L.A.의 상사 같지 않게...'
여기서 who는 boss의 주격 관계대명사이다.

CHOOSE YOUR ATTITUDE— *I think we have a good start on this one. The menu idea the staff came up with was terrific; the first real sign of progress.*

Without choose your attitude, all the rest is a waste of time. I need to continue exploring and expanding our awareness of this ingredient.

PLAY— *the fish market is an adult playground. If the fish guys can have that much fun selling fish, there is hope for us at First Guarantee.*

MAKE THEIR DAY— *Customers are encouraged to play also. The atmosphere is one of inclusion. Not at all like the boss I had in L.A who talked to me like I was a tape recorder and never shared any of the interesting work.*

BE PRESENT— *The fish guys are fully present. They are not daydreaming or on the phone. They are scanning the crowed and interacting with customers. They talk to me as if I was a long lost friend.*

converse 대화를 나누다 **distinct** 구별되는, 특이한 **odor** 냄새 **emanate** 흘러나오다 **hint** 암시 **hang up the phone** 전화를 끊다 **stand up** 대항하다 **intimidate** 겁주다, 위협하다 **field trip** 현장견학

· · ·

the hint of a smile in his voice '웃는다는 것을 알 수 있는 그의 목소리'
But if you can make me smile with the day I have ahead, you may be on to something. 'the day I have ahead'는 '내 앞에 있는 하루' 즉, '오늘 하루'를 말한다. 그리고 'be on to'는 구어적 표현으로 '뭔가를 알고 있다'는 뜻이다. 따라서 이 문장을 해석하면 '당신이 오늘 하루 나를 웃게 만들 수 있다면, 당신은 뭔가를 알고 있을 것이다'

· · ·

We're just friends
우린 그저 친구 사이죠

미국인들의 우정과 한국인들의 우정은 그 개념이 전혀 다르다. 미국인들은 모르는 사람에게도 'Hi'라고 쉽게 인사한다. 이것은 친밀감를 나타내는 것이 아니라 하나의 습관이다. 미국사회는 동적인 사회이기 때문에 우정을 쌓는 것이 참 힘든 사회이다. 사실 Pay(급여)가 좋지 않으면 오랫동안 다닌 직장이더라도 미련 없이 떠난다. 그래서 그들은 friends(친구), close friends(친한 친구)를 구별한다.

Monday Morning

As she entered the elevator, she noticed Bill right behind her. That will save me the trip to his office, she thought. The car was crowded so they didn't converse, but when the door opened on her floor, she turned to Bill and handed her boss her bag, which had a distinct order emanating from it. "A gift, Bill. It's called a smiling sushi." As the door closed she heard a loud, "Mary Jane!"

A Few seconds after she was at her desk the phone rang. "Strange gift, Mary Jane. I don't know what a fish market has o do with First Guarantee, But if you can make me smile with the day I have ahead, you may be on to something."

When she hung up he phone, she was aware that her relationship with Bill was somehow different.

I didn't think many on his staff stand up to him. She thought, Strange as it seems, I believe he appreciates the fact that I have chosen not to de intimidated.

The Field Trip

At the first of her two Monday morning staff meetings

get right to the point 바로 요점으로 들어가다 **objec-tion** 반대 **rearrange** 다시 배열하다

• • •

Brown bag lunch 갈색 종이봉투에 담아 오는 간단한 음식을 말한다. 미국에서는 brown bag lunch(meeting) '간단히 점심을 먹으면서 하는 세미나'라는 뜻으로 많이 쓰인다.

it's the talking of the building '그것은 건물의 화제거리다'

guys there who have solved their version of our problem '우리의 문제를 그들의 방식으로 해결한 사람들' 여기서 'guys'는 남자들이라는 뜻이 아니라 사람들을 친근하게 지칭하는 구어적 표현이다.

The voices of those around her rose with objections. '반대와 함께 그러한 목소리가 커졌다'

she got right to the point. "I'm impressed and heartened by how you have worked at finding ways to remind us all that we can choose our attitude each day, The Choose Your Attitude Menu was a great idea, and it's the talk of he building. It's fun at last to hear some positive comments. Now it's time to take the next step. There is something I want you all to experience, so we are going on a lunchtime field trip. This group will go on Wednesday, the other group on Thursday. Brown bag lunches will be provided, so just bring yourselves.

"The field trip will be to a place many of you have visited before. We are going to a special fish market where you will study energy in action. There are a bunch of guys there who have solved their version of our problem. It will be our task to see if we can understand and apply their secrets for success."

"I have a dental appointment." "I have plans for lunch that day." The voices of those around her rose with objections. She was surprised when she heard a strong voice, her own, say, "I expect you all to be there and to rearrange your plans to make that possible. This is important."

On Wednesday, the first group met in the lobby and

head for ~로 향하다 **observe** 관찰하다 **chuckle** 킬킬 웃다 **handy** 바로 쓸 수 있는 **quote** 인용 **polite** 정중한 **disperse** 흩어지게 하다 **obviously** 명백히, 분명히 **initiative** 시작, 솔선, 독창력 **most likely** 모르면 몰라도 **brief** 간단히 알리다, 요약하다 **be reserved** 조심성이 많다, 서먹서먹하다 **slip** 미끄러지다 **grasp** 움켜잡다

• • •

Good for John and Steve, she thought. Great initiative. 'Good for'는 칭찬할 때 사용하는 표현이다. 이 문장을 해석하면 'John과 Steve가 잘하고 있군, 시작이 멋진데'

...the group was rather reserved until something special happened. '그 그룹은 어떤 특별한 일이 생길 때까지 오히려 조심스러웠다'

134

headed for the market. "All I want you to do is observe the scene you are about to see." She chuckled, "Be sure to keep your yogurt handy." Her use of the Yogi Berra quote, "You can observe a lot by watching," received one polite laugh. Well, it's a start, she thought.

The fish market was busy when they arrived, and they quickly dispersed. That made it hard for her to watch reactions, but she did notice a few of her staff obviously enjoying themselves. She saw John and Steve in close conversation with one of the fish guys and moved closer to observe. "When you are present with people you look right at them...just like being with you best friend... everything is going on around you but you're still taking care of just them," said the redheaded fish guy to John.

Good for John and Steve, she thought. Great initiative.

On Thursday the second group made the trip, most likely briefed by the first group. There were almost no questions, and the group was rather reserved until something special happened. Stephanie, a longtime employee, was asked if she wanted to go behind the counter and catch a fish. Although she had seemed quite shy at work, she accepted. Two fish slipped through her grasp, much to the delight of the crowd and the special

amusement 즐거움 **dazzle** 감탄시키다 **bare-handed** 맨손 **thunderous** 우
뢰 같은 **applause** 박수 **catcall** 날카로운 휘파람 **whistle** 휘파람 **gang** 한 무
리 **overhead** 머리 위로 **neat** 산뜻한, 멋진 **nod** 끄덕임 **pass through** 지나
가다 **protest** 항의하다, 이의를 제기하다 **contribute** 기여하다 **wisecracker**
재치 있게 말하는 사람

· · ·

She was hooked as the fish guys made her day. '그녀는 어상인들이 그녀
의 날을 만들어 주자 사로잡혔다' 여기에 hook은 수동의 형태로 '사로잡히다'
라는 뜻이 된다. 또한 as는 '~하자마자' 라는 뜻으로 쓰였다.

Then reality set in. '현실이 밀려오기 시작했다'

In both groups, protest followed the intial smiles. '두 그룹 모두 처음의
웃음을 뒤로하고 항의했다'

amusement of her coworkers. On the third try, she made a dazzling bare-handed catch which was followed by thunderous applause, catcalls and whistles. She was hooked as the fish guys made her day.

Stephanie seemed to open the door for others. As the fish flew overhead, the gang from First Guarantee did a lot more than raise their yogurt cups in the air.

Friday Afternoon Meetings

On Friday afternoon, she met with each group separately. "Wouldn't it be neat to work in a place where you could have as much fun as the guys do at the Pike Place Fish market?" she asked. There were a few nods and some smiles as the image of a flying fish passed through their minds. Stephanie had the biggest smile of all. Then reality set in.

In both groups, protest followed the initial smiles. "We don't sell fish!" Mark said. "We don't have anything to throw," added Beth. "It's guy thing," contributed Ann. "Our work is boring," said another. One wisecracker said, "Let's throw the purchase orders."

"You're right; this isn't a fish market; what we do is

look forward to ~을 기대하다 **demonstrate** 증명하다 **take it further** 그
이상의 조치를 취하다 **morgue** 시체공시소, 음침한 곳 **raise** 키우다

different. What I'm asking is: Are you interested in having a place to work which has as much energy as the world famous Pike Place Fish market? A place where you smile more often. A place where you have positive feelings about what you do and the way do it. A place you look forward to being at each day. You've already demonstrated that in many ways we can choose our attitude. Are you interested in taking it further?"

Stephanie spoke up. "I like the people here; they're good people. But I hate coming to work. I can hardly breathe in this place. It's like a morgue. So I might as well admit it: I've been looking for another job. If we could find a way to create some life here, it would be a more satisfying place to work, and I would definitely consider staying."

"Thank you for your honesty and courage, Stephanie."

Steve added, "I want to make this place more fun." Randy raised his hand.

"Yes, Randy?"

"You talked about your personal situation the other day, Mary Jane. I never heard a boss do that before and it got me thinking. I'm raising my son alone, and I need this job and the benefits that go with it. I don't like to make

take out 분풀이하다 **frustration** 좌절, 낙담 **trap** (덫 등으로) 잡다, 가두다
gratitude 감사 **add** 덧붙이다 **contribution** 공헌, 기여 **stimulate** 자극하
다, 격려하다 **pop up** 갑자기 나타나다

· · ·

I'm sorry to admit. '나는 인정하기 싫지만' 인정하는 것이 유감이지만 인정
해야 한다는 뜻.

They seem to have it so good, while I'm trapped here in this pit. '내가 이
구덩이에 잡혀 있는 동안, 그들은 너무 좋은 것을 가지고 있는 것처럼 보인다'

140

waves, but I'm sorry to admit I sometimes take out my frustrations on people in other departments. They seem to have it so good, while I'm trapped here in this pit. You're helped me realize that we make this place in pit by the way we act here. Well, if we can choose to make it a pit, them we can also choose something else. The thought of doing that has me really excited. If I can learn to have fun and be happy here, well, them I guess I can also learn to do that in other parts of my life."

"Thanks, Randy." She turned and looked directly at him with gratitude, adding, "I see a few heads nodding, and I know you're said something really important here today. You have touched me and others with your words from the heart. Thank you for your contribution. Let's build a better workplace, a place we love to be in.

"On Monday we'll start the process of putting the Fish Philosophy to work on the third floor. Between now and then, I want you to think about your personal experience at the fish market and write down any questions or ideas you have. When we get together next time, we can discuss how to proceed. Just let what you saw at the market stimulate your thinking."

The wisecracker popped up again, "Well, if we can't

confetti 색종이 조각 **shredder** 서류 분쇄기 **outline** 개요, 윤곽 **walk through** 대강 마치다 **retreat** 물러나다 **exhaust** 소진시키다, 고갈시키다 **impatient** 성급한, 참지 못하는

• • •

Little did she know that half a dozen of her employees would find a reason to visit the market again that weekend... '그녀는 직원들 중 6명이나 주말에 시장을 다시 찾아갈 이유를 발견할 거라고는 전혀 생각하지 못했다' little이 문장의 맨 앞에 놓이면 '전혀~못하다'라는 부정의 의미로 쓰인다. 주로 동사 'think, know, suspect'와 함께 많이 쓰인다.

142

throw the purchase orders paper, can't we at least throw the confetti from the shredder?" Laughter filled the room. That feels good, she thought.

Mary Jane then passed copies of an outline she had developed at the market and walked everyone through her personal observations. She encouraged her staff to remember and record their own thoughts over the weekend.

After the second meeting ended, Mary Jane retreated to her office and sat exhausted at her desk. I gave them something to think about over the weekend. But will they? Little did she know that half a dozen of her employees would find a reason to visit the market again that weekend, many of them with family and friends.

MARY JANE'S OUTLINE

Choose Your Attitude—The fish guys are aware that they choose their attitude each day. One of the fish guys said, "When you are doing what you are doing, who are you being" Are you being impatient and bored, or are you being world famous? You are doing to act

differently 다르게 **energize** 힘을 주다, 격려하다 **goodwill** 호의, 친절

• • •

Please bring your thoughts with you on Monday. '월요일에 당신의 생각을 적어내세요' 여기서 bring은 '적어내다' 정도로 해석하는 것이 좋다.

differently if you are being world famous." Who do we want to be while we do our work?

Play—The fish guys have fun while they work, and fun is energizing. How could we have more fun and create more energy?

Make their day—The fish guys include the customers in their good time. They engage their customers in ways which create energy and goodwill. Who are our customers and how can we engage them in a way that will make their day? How could we make each other's days?

Be Present—The fish guys are fully present at work. What can they teach us about being for each other and our customers?

Please bring your thoughts
With you on Monday.
MJR

assignment 숙제, 할당 simultaneously 동시에, 일제히 drown out 안 들리게 하다 accent 억양 above all 무엇보다도 commotion 동요, 소동 a bit of 조금, 작은 mystery 비밀, 수수께끼

• • •

No wonder they' re so good at being present... 'no wonder'은 '당연하다'는 뜻으로 '그들이 현재에 충실하기에 능숙한 것은 당연해' 라고 해석한다.
You seem puzzled. '당신 곤혹스러워 보이는군요' puzzle은 '수수께끼'라는 의미로 많이 쓰이지만 수동형으로 쓰면 '곤혹스럽다, 난처하다' 라는 의미로도 쓰인다.

• • •

I was wondering if you could help me?

저를 도와주시겠습니까?

시제가 과거형이지만 과거와는 무관한 표현으로 상대방에게 불쾌감을 주지 않고 조심스럽게 제안을 할 때 쓰는 표현이다.

That Weekend at the Fish Market

"Teacher give you an assignment?"

Stephanie looked up and simultaneously saw a fish fly through the air and Lonnie's smiling face. "Hi. I guess you might say my boss gave me some homework."

"That wouldn't be Mary Jane, would it?"

"How did you know?" Her response was drowned out by a monger shouting, "Three tuna flying away to hear her anyway. No wonder they're so good at being present, she thought. They have to be if they want to hear anything above all this commotion.

"I saw you here during the week with Mary Jane's group. You are also the first yogurt dude I remember catching a fish as long as I've been here."

"Really?"

"So how can I help you? You seem puzzled."

She looked down at her notes. "I think I understand be present, the way you are right now with me. And when I was catching the fish—well... I will never forget the way you made my day. Play is something that comes easy for me—I love to enjoy myself and fool around. But choose your attitude is still a bit of a mystery. I mean, doesn't your

professional 전문적인 **cute** 귀여운 **introduction** 소개 **vow** 맹세하다, 서약하다 **take off** 떠나다, 벗다 **sip** 조금씩 마시다 **muffin** (둥근 모양의)빵 **guarantee** 보장, 보증

· · ·

Wolf was on his way to a career as a professional race car driver... '울프는 전문 레이서로 일을 하러가는 도중이었다' 'on one's way to'는 '~하러 가는 도중에'라는 뜻의 숙어이다.

attitude have a lot to do with the way you are treated and what happens to you?"

"I know just the person you need to ask about attitude: Wolf. Wolf was on his way to a career as a professional race car driver when he had a serious accident. Well, I' ll let Wolf tell the story. We need to go back into the locker. Will you be warm enough?"

"Can we come, too?"

Stephanie looked to her left and saw Steve, Randy, and one very cute child. After introductions, they all went back to talk to Wolf, who told them how, while he was recovering from his accident, he learned to choose his attitude every day. His vowed to share them with their fellow workers at the Monday meeting.

Afterward, Steve had to take off, but Stephanie, Randy, and Randy's son went across the street to a cafe. The adults sipped coffee, while Randy's son ate a giant chocolate chip muffin.

"You know," said Stephanie, "we might as well clean up our toxic energy dump because there is no guarantee the next job will be any different. And think about it. How many bosses are there like Mary Jane? I really respect her. Think about what she's been through. I hear she even stood

bully 약자를 괴롭히는 사람, 골목대장 **count for** 가치 있다 **skeptical** 회의 석인, 의심 많은 **scare** 겁내다, 놀라다 **get better** 더 나아지다 **unfold** 펼치 다 **buzz** 소음, 와글와글(하는 소리) **assemble** 모으다, 집합하다

· · ·

...the sky is the limit for us with a boss like Mary Jane 'the sky is the limit' 직역하면 '하늘이 한계'라는 뜻으로 그 만큼 한계가 없다는 뜻이다. '제 한은 없다, 얼마든지 할 수 있다'는 뜻의 관용표현으로 쓰인다.
The plan unfolds '계획을 펼치다'

· · ·

Give me a buzz.
전화를 주십시오.

가끔씩 TV를 보면 '부저를 눌러 주세요'라는 말을 들을 수 있다. 이는 영어 buzzer로 '사이렌'을 뜻한다. buzz는 이러한 사이렌에서 나오는 소리이다. 전 화가 울릴 때도 비슷한 소리가 나기 때문에 미국에서는 (구어로)전화를 buzz라 고 지칭하기도 한다.

up to that jerk Bill Walsh. None of the other department managers ever stood up to that bully. I mean that counts for something, doesn't it, Randy?"

"Stephanie, you're reading my mind. If these fish guys could do what they have done, the sky is the limit for us with a boss like Mary Jane. It isn't going to be easy, some of our coworkers are as frightened as I used to be. They're skeptical because they're scared. Perhaps if we provide a positive example it will help. All I know is that things won't get better until we choose to make tem better ? and I want things to get better."

As Stephanie walked to her car she noticed betty and her husband. She waved and then became aware of three other people from her office in the crowd. Great! She thought.

The Plan Unfolds

There was a buzz in the room as the first group assembled for the Monday morning meeting. Mary Jane opened the meeting by saying, "We're here to clean up what has been called a toxic energy dump. Today we'll see if we have any additional lessons from the market and

move on 계속 앞으로 나아가다 jump to one's feet 벌떡 일어서다 take turn 교대하다 recall 생각해내다, 소환하다 scary 무서운 growl 으르렁거리다 turn away 외면하다 freak 이상한 wallow 몸부림치다, 빠지다 in pity 연민, 동정 slip away 지나가다 a series of 일련의 miss 놓치다 opportunity 기회 be fascinated with ~에 매혹되다

. . .

Stephanie and Randy jumped to their feet and took turns recalling their conversation with Wolf. '스테파니와 랜디는 벌떡 일어서서 교대로 울프와의 대화를 생각해냈다'

...he could let life slip away in a series of missed opportunities. 여기서 'let'은 '~하게 내버려두다'로 해석할 수 있다. 이 문장을 해석하면 '그는 놓쳐버린 기회들 속에서 삶이 지나가게 내버려 둘 수도 있었다'

then decide on our next steps. Did anyone think of anything during the weekend that we should consider before moving on?

Stephanie and Randy jumped to their feet and took turns recalling their conversation with Wolf. Stephanie began.

"Wolf was really cool, although he was a little scary at first. I mean his voice is like a growl. Anyway, he told us his story of having a career as a professional race car driver torn away from him by a freak accident. He said he wallowed in pity for a while and then, when his girlfriend left him and friends stopped calling, he realized he had a basic choice to live fully every day since. It was quite a story."

"My son was fascinated with Wolf," continued Randy. "Wolf really got me thinking about our situation here on three, and how much power we have over the kind of place we create. We could make three into a great place to work if we learn the lesson of Wolf. We must choose our attitude every day and choose it well."

Steve also offered some observations.

"Thanks, Steve. Thank you, Randy. Thanks, Stephanie. It sound like you were busy this weekend. And thanks for

ask for 청구하다 **overtime** 초과근무 **die down** 차차 진정되다 **nod** 끄덕임 **sign up** 등록하다 **prefer** 선호하다 **go along** ~에 찬성하다 **pass around** 나누어 주다 **relieve** 안도하게 하다 **concrete** 구체적인 **volunteer** 자원자 **gentle** 상냥한, 온화한 **negotiate** 협상하다, 교섭하다 **genuine** 진짜의, 성실한

· · ·

Mary Jane decided to bring the discussion to a close. '메리 제인은 토론을 끝내기로 결심했다' 'bring to a close'는 '끝내다'라는 뜻의 숙어이다.

not asking for overtime!" After the laughter died down, Mary Jane asked, "Who else has something to offer which will help us understand these points?" Forty-five minutes later, Mary Jane decided to bring the discussion to a close. "Any ideas on where we go from here?"

"Why don't we from a team for each of the four ingredients? said one of the newer employees.

There were a number of nods.

"All right," said Mary Jane. "Let me make sure the other half agrees with this approach. Why don't you sign up for the group you prefer; if the other group goes along, I will put everything in memo form and get it to you tomorrow. Is there anything else to discuss?"

At the end of the meeting she passed around a sign-up sheet and asked each of them to sign up for one of the four teams. The second group fully supported the idea of teams and seemed relieved to have a concrete plan of action.

The teams go to work

The Play Team had a few too many volunteers, so Mary Jane did a little gentle negotiating, "I have a genuine Pike Place Fish market T-shirt for the first three volunteers

put together (하나로) 합하다, 종합적으로 판단하다 expectation 기대, 예상 additional 추가적인 off-site 떨어진(특정한곳에서) implementation 이행, 실행 be responsible for ～에 책임이 있다 arrangement 배열 budget 예산 discretion 재량

who will move from play to Choose Your Attitude or Be Present." Once the teams were balanced, she put together a memo with the general guidelines and expectations.

Team Guidelines

- Teams will have six weeks to meet, study their topic, collect additional information, and put together a presentation that will be made to the group as a whole at and off-site meeting.

- Each presentation must have some action items that we can consider for implementation.

- Teams will be responsible for setting their own meeting times and may use two hours of work time each week for team business. Arrangements must be made to cover the work of those at team meetings during business hours.

- Each team has a budget of $200 to be spent at its discretion.

facilitate 용이하게 하다, 촉진하다 **be available** 이용가능한 **troubleshot** 중재 **impasse** 막다른 골목, 곤경 **essential** 가장 중요한 **function** 기능 **organize** 조직하다 **sense** 감지하다 **level** 수준, 단계 **keep up** 유지하다

• • •

Bill surprised her by offering to help personally as well as organize the coverage. '빌은 대신 근무 서는 것을 준비해줄 뿐만 아니라 개인적인 도움을 제안해 그녀를 놀라게 했다. corerage는 '적용범위'라는 뜻이지만 여기서는 문맥상 '대신 근무 서는 것의 정도나 범위'로 이해하면 된다.

- Teams will facilitate their own meetings.

- I will be available to troubleshoot if the team reaches an impasse, but I would rather the team work out its issues as a team.

Good Luck! Let's create a place where we all want to work!

MJR

Team Reports

Six weeks had passed since the teams started meeting. The presentations would be made today. Mary Jane had asked Bill if people from other departments could handle essential functions for a morning, so the whole group could meet; Bill surprised her by offering to help personally as well as organize the coverage, "I don't know what you're doing," he said, "but I already sense a new level of energy on three. Keep up the good work and let me know if there is anything else I can do."

nervous 긴장되는, 불안한 **supportive** 지지하는, 격려하는 **request** 요청하
다 **specific** 세부사항 **ap-propriate** 적절하다 **underlie** ~의 기초가 되다
surge 파도

· · ·

**I want the ingredient that underlies all of the others to be last thing we
consider.** '나는 다른 것들의 기본이 되는 요소는 우리가 고려할 가장 마지막
것이 되기를 원합니다'

She was a bit nervous. Each of the teams had asked her to meet with them at least once, and she had done her best to be helpful and supportive without taking control. Although she had been asked for reading material and the use of a conference room in the last two weeks, none of the teams had requested more than that. She really didn' t have a clue about the specifics of any of the four presentations. And today was the day they would go off-site to hear the teams reports.

At nine in the morning, they all walked down to the Alexis Hotel as Bill and the other volunteers arrived to cover the office. "Good luck," he sail.

They arrived at the Alexis and were directed to the Market Room. Appropriate, she thought. She had decided that the Choose Your Attitude Team should present last. Sha had explained to each team: "I want the ingredient that underlies all of the others to be the last thing we consider,"

She felt a surge of emotion as she entered the meeting room. The room was a sea of color, music, and energy. Balloons were attached to each chair, and colorful flower arrangements brought the room to life. They have responded to the challenge, she thought. Their clocks are

come up 걸어오다, 다가오다 **awkwardly** 어색하게 **spokesperson** 대변인
sort of 일종의 **cakewalk** 미국 남부의 흑인들로부터 비롯된 춤

· · ·

He's playing a cat and mouse game with us.
그는 우리를 농락하고 있어.

'톰과 제리'처럼 앙숙인 고양이와 쥐의 관계에 비유한 표현이다.

wound up again. The biggest surprise of the day was sitting in the back of the room in his full fishmonger outfit. It was Lonnie. She took the seat next to him as things began.

The Play Team

One of the members of the Play Team called the room to attention and asked the whole staff to come up front. As directions were given, everyone stood around rather awkwardly. "Our report is in the form of a game which we' ll all play," said Betty, the Play Team spokesperson.

The Play Team had designed a game using a path of circles cut from colored paper and arranged on the floor so you could step from one circle to the next as the music played. Each circle had written on it a key point from their report. When the music stopped, the person standing on a specific circle was asked to read the text on it. It was sort of like a cakewalk. There were two group of items. One was a list of benefits and the other a list of implementation ideas. Great work, thought Mary Jane.

bulletin board 게시판 **aquarium** 수족관 **lighten up** 느긋해지다

· · ·

Work becomes a reward and not just a way to rewards. '일은 단지 보상의 수단이 아니라 보상 그 자체가 된다'

Small lights to turn on when it is time to lighten up a bit or when you have a good idea. '느긋해질 필요가 있거나, 좋은 아이디어가 생겼을 때 켤 작은 조명들' 'lighten up'은 기본적으로 '완화하다', '늦추다'의 의미이고 이것은 표현은 'relax', 'take it easy'와 같은 의미이다.

164

Benefit of Play

- Happy people treat others well.
- Fun leads to creativity.
- The time passes quickly
- Having a good time is healthy.
- Work becomes a reward and not just a way to rewards.

Implementing Play on the Third Floor

- Post signs saying, THIS IS A PLAYGROUND. WATCH OUT FOR ADULT CHILDREN.
- Start a joke-of-the-month contest with its own bulletin board.
- Add more color and make the environment more interesting.
- Add more life with plants and an aquarium.
- Special events such as a lunchtime comedian.
- Small lights to turn on when it is time to lighten up a bit or when you have a good idea.

designate 명시하다, 지명하다 **ongoing** 진행 중 **committee** 위원회 **divide into** ~로 나누다 **assignment** 할당, 숙제 **mill around** 오락가락하다 **survey** 조사 **perform** 이행하다, 실행하다 **audible** 들리는 **gasp** (공포, 놀람 등으로)숨 막힘

- Instruction in creativity.
- A designated creativity area called the Sand Box.
- Form an ongoing play committee to keep the idea flowing.

The Make Their Day Team

The Make Their Day Team Was next. "Go out into the hall and have some coffee while we set up," was their first instruction. When everyone was called back into the room, the staff was divided into small groups with a member of the Make Their Day Team in each group. Stephanie described the assignment as everyone milled around.

"I want each group to take fifteen minutes to develop a list of strategies for supporting and enhancing the work of a key group of people, our internal customers. But first I want to introduce some data. These are the findings of a customer survey we performed. Take a deep breath because you aren't going to like what you see." A side went up. A wave of shock passed through the room; there was actually one audible gasp.

dread 꺼리다 **sleepwalker** 몽유병환자 **sedate** 차분한, 침착한 **impersonal** 비인간적인 **treatment** 취급 **adequate** 충분한, 알맞은 **rarely** 좀처럼 ~하지 않는 **interrupt** 방해하다 **convey** 나르다, 운반하다 **attempt** 시도하다 **thereof** 그것에 대해, 그것으로부터 **stampede** 앞 다투어 달아남 **commitment** 헌신 **enterprise** 회사

• • •

Our customer joke about our response, or lack thereof, to a problem which arises after 4. '우리 고객들은 4시 이후에 발생하는 문제들에 대한 우리의 반응 혹은 반응 없음에 대해 농담을 한다'

We do our job, period, and on more. '우리는 우리의 일을 할 뿐 그 이상은 하지 않는다' 여기서 period는 '마침표'라는 뜻으로 쓰였으며 '할 일을 하는 것으로 끝이다' 라는 의미이다.

RESULTS OF CUSTOMER SURVEY

1. Our customers dread working with us. They call us "the sleepwalkers" because we seen positively sedated to them. They would prefer a good fight than the impersonal treatment they receive.

2. The work we do is adequate, but we rarely offer to extent ourselves in order to help them serve the external customer. We do our job, period, and no more.

3. We often treat our customer as if they are interrupting us.

4. We frequently pass our customers around from one person to another without ever conveying an interest in solving the problem. We appear to be attempting to avoid responsibility.

5. Our customer joke about our response, or lack there of, to a problem which arises after 4. They laugh about the stampede to the elevator at 4:30.

6. Our customers question our very commitment to the enterprise.

7. We are referred to ad the "last stage of decline."

contractor 계약자 spin 돌리다 considerable 상당한, 고려할 만한 count
on 의지하다, 기대하다 obligation 의무, 책임 compensation 보수, 봉급
impediment 방해, 장애

• • •

...when we drop the ball or drag our feet '우리가 실수하거나, 일을 지연
시킬 때' 'drop the ball'은 '실수하다', 'drag one's feet'은 '일을 지연시키
다' 라는 뜻의 관용 표현이다.

• • •

You are bad news.

너만 보면 기분이 나빠.

미국에서는 늘 말썽(trouble)만 피우고 골치 아픈 대상을 가리켜 'bad news'
라는 표현을 사용한다.

170

8. Discussions have started concerning the possibility of replacing our department with an outside contractor.

Stephanie said, "Our team was first shocked and then angered by these findings. Slowly we came to realize that the customers feel how they feel. No matter what excuses we offer or what kind of spin we put on it, it doesn't change how our internal customers feel. That's the reality as they see it. The question is, what are we going to do about it?

Another team member continued with considerable passion, "I don't think we realize how important our role is in the business of First Guarantee. Many people count on us, and they look bad when we drop the ball or drag our feet. The fact that many of us have other obligations and that we aren't very high on the compensation scale is not their problem. They're just trying to serve the customers who pay our salaries — and we're seen by them as an impediment to high quality service."

Then Stephanie said, "We need your ideas and need

come up with 생각해내다 **scribe** 서기 **integrate** 통합하다 **reconvene** 다시 소집하다 **summary** 요약, 개요 **focus onto** ~에 초점을 맞추다

· · ·

...still riding on the energy generated by the first presentation '첫 번째 발표로 인해 발생한 에너지에 여전히 편승하여'

them badly. Please help us to take a step away from the dump and toward making our customers' day. Each group has forty-five minutes to come up with as many ideas as possible. Please find a seat and get started. The member of our team will serve as scribe." There was silence for a while. Then the groups began attacking the problem, still riding on the energy generated by the first presentation.

When the time had come, Stephanie announced, "Let's take a short break while the scribes integrate their notes." After ten minutes, she reconvened the staff. "Here's a quick look at the results," she said, "and this award goes to the members of the table four group." The people from table four came up to receive their Make Their Day buttons. Smaller buttons were passed out to everyone else. Attention turned to their summary report.

Benefits of Make Their Day

- It is good for business
- Serving our customers well give us the satisfaction that comes to those who serve other. It will focus our attention, away from our problems onto how we can

unleash 해방하다, 자유롭게 하다 **stagger** 시차제를 두다 **coverage** 적용범위 **category** 범주, 구분 **annual** 1년의 **recommendation** 추천 **appoint** 지명하다, 임명하다 **task force** 특별 팀 **dedicate** 바치다, 봉헌하다

• • •

A.M.과 P.M. 'A.M: ante meridiem = before noon', 'P.M: post meridiem = after midday' a.m.을 쓸 때는 꼭 숫자 뒤에 써야 하며, p.m.을 쓸 때는 o'clock과 함께 쓰지 않는다.
360-degree feedback 모든 방향으로부터의 반응, 의견

make a positive difference to others. This is healthy, will feel good, and will unleash even more energy.

Implementing Make Their Day

- Stagger our hours so there is coverage from 7 A.M. until 6 P.M. This will be good for our customers(and may also be helpful to some of us who need different start times).

- Pull together some focus groups to study ways we can be of service to our customers. Should we have specialty groups, for instance, focusing on specific customer categories?

- Have a monthly and an annual award for service, based on the recommendation of our customers who said their day had been made.

- Implement a 360-degree feedback process which includes our customers.

- Appoint a special task force dedicated to surprising and delighting our customer.

- Ask our key customers to "come out and play" once a month.

SAS Scandinavian Airline System **transaction** 처리, 취급 **rejoice** 기뻐하다, 좋아하다 **turn around** (태도를)일변하다 **pace** 속도 **soothing** 위로하는, 진정하는 **visualization** 시각화

- Study what it would take to implement the "moment of truth" idea, which started at SAS, Scandanavian Airlines. We would try to make every transaction with our customers a positive transaction.

Mary Jane quietly rejoiced. "If they care this much, we can turn our department around. Stephanie is on fire and her group shows signs of catching the same enthusiasm. We can do it! I know we can!" Out of the corner of her eye she noticed that Lonnie had a pleased look on his face.

The Present Moment Team

The Present Moment Team took and entirely different approach, which gave a welcome change of pace. With soothing music playing in the background, one of the group members said, "Close your eyes and relax for a minute. Breathe deeply as I guide you through a number of visualizations that will help us be fully present."

When she was finished, she said, "Now listen as members of our group offer some thoughts. Stay relaxed,

inspirational 영감을 불러일으키는　**catch up** 따라붙다　**urgent** 긴급한
choke 숨 막히게 하다 **pause** 잠시 멈추다, 중단하다

· · ·

try to even your breathing 여기서 'even'은 '고르게 하다'라는 뜻의 동사
로 사용되었다. 이 문장을 해석하면 '호흡을 고르게 하려고 노력하세요'
...trying to make ends meet and working both sides against the middle.
'make ends meet'는 '수입에 맞게 생활하다'라는 뜻이고 'against the
middle'은 중간이 아닌 즉, '최선을 다했다'는 뜻이다.
**His daughter is now fifteen and no longer interested in the park, nor,
for that matter, in him.** '그의 딸은 이제 15살이고 더 이상 공원에도, 관심
없기로 말하자면, 그에게도 관심 없었다' 'for that matter'는 '그 일을 말할 것
같으면'이라는 의미의 관용 표현이다.

try to even your breathing, and keep your eyes closed."

A number of inspirational readings followed. One of the readings went something like this:

The past is history
The future is a mystery
Today is a gift
That is why we call it the present

John offered a personal story. "I was living a busy life," he said with sadness in his voice, "trying to make ends meet and working both sides against the middle. One day my daughter asked me to go to the park. I told her it was a wonderful idea, but I had a lot to do at that moment. I said she should wait until later, after I had a chance to catch up. But there always seemed to be some urgent and pressing work to do and the days passed. days led to weeks and weeks to months." With a choking voice, he said that four years passed and he never did go to the park. His daughter is now fifteen and no longer interested in the park, nor, for that matter, in him.

John paused and took a deep breath. "I talked to one of the fish guys about being present, and I realized how

infrequently 드물게, 어쩌다 **wear down** 조금씩 공격하여 무너뜨리다
dedicate 헌신하다 **distract** (주의를)딴 데로 돌리다

· · ·

He was higher than a kite ever since. '그는 그 이후 연보다 더 높이 떠있었
다' 우리가 기분이 좋을 때 '마음이 붕 뜬다'고 표현하는 것과 마찬가지로 기
분이 매우 좋은 상태를 의미하는 표현이다.

· · ·

I was hoping you might take a look at my report.
당신이 내 보고서를 검토해줬으면 좋겠어요.

우리는 부탁이나 요청을 표현할 때 주로 'I hope~'를 쓰는데 미국인들은 'I
was hoping~'으로 많이 쓴다. 과거시제가 사용된 이유는 희망하는 사실이
이미 과거부터 마음속에 있었다는 사실을 의미하기 때문이다. 그만큼 부탁이
나 요청을 꼭 들어줬으면 좋겠다는 뉘앙스를 담고 있다.

infrequently I was really present at home or at work. The fish guy invited me to visit the market with the whole family. My daughter didn't want to go, but I finally wore her down and she came along. We had a good time, and I worked on being present with my children. When my wife took my son down the street to the toy store, I sat down with my daughter and told her how sorry I was that I really hadn't been there for her. I told her I hoped she could forgive me and that while I couldn't change the past, I let her know that I was now dedicated to being present in the present. She said I wasn't that bad a dad — I just needed to lighten up a little. I've got a ways to go," he said, "but I'm improving. Being present could help me recover something I wasn't aware I had lost: a relationship with my daughter."

After John was finished, Lonnie whispered to Mary Jane, "The fish guy was Jacob. He has been higher than a kite ever since. He's a new guy, and it was his first taste of really helping someone."

Janet also became quite emotional when she described a coworker at her previous job. "This person kept trying to get my attention," she said, "but I was distracted by personal issues, and we never connected. Then all hell

reach out ~을 얻으려고 노력하다 **all hell break loose** 대혼란에 빠지다
stationary bike 페달 밟는 운동기구 **distress** 괴롭히다, 고민하게 하다
efficiency 능률 **set aside** 옆에 두다 **cope with** 대처하다 **confirm** (결심 등
을)굳게 하다

• • •

**It seems she was way over her head and was covering up the lack of
progress by issuing imaginary reports.** '그녀는 너무 어려워 하는 것으로
보였고 진행의 지연을 감추기 위해 가짜 보고서를 제출했다' 'way over one's
head'는 '너무 어렵다'는 뜻의 관용 표현이다. 그리고 issue는 보통 '쟁점'이
라는 명사로 쓰이지만 여기서는 '발행하다, 제출하다'라는 뜻의 동사로 쓰였다.

broke loose. It seems she was way over her head and was covering up the lack of progress by issuing imaginary reports. By the time it all came to light, it was too late to correct. She lost her job, the company lost a client and a great deal of money, and I eventually lost my job because we unable to replace the work. All of this could have been avoided if I had been present for a coworker who was reaching out for help."

Then Beth told a personal story of riding on a stationary bike in front of the TV while trying to catch up on some reading, when her son came in and sat down on the couch. She could tell he was distressed. "A mother knows these things," she said. "In the past I would have continued doing what I was doing while talking to him. But experience and a divorce have taught me that efficiency isn't always wise or nice with loved ones. So I turned off the TV, got off of the bicycle, set the magazines aside, and spent the next hour listening deeply as my son described the difficult time he was having just coping with life. I was really glad I made the choice to be fully present."

A few more members of the group told a mix of personal and business stories. Then they confirmed their commitment to bring present for one another and for

code phrase 약속 어구　**signal** 신호　**verbal** 구두의　**accountability** 책임
proactivity 주도성

internal customers. "When you are present you show consideration for the other person," one of the team members added. They also committed to being fully present when discussing and issue, whether with each other or a customer; they would truly listen and not allow themselves to be distracted. They encouraged one another to ask, "Is this a good time? Are you present?" To support one another in asking these questions they established a code phrase. "You seem distracted," was chosen as a special code to signal a possible present moment issue. Everyone agreed to give it a try. And everyone also agreed never again to read or answer e-mails while talking on the phone with a colleague or customer.

The Choose Your Attitude Team

Last came the Choose Your Attitude Team. Their verbal report was brief and to the point. "Here are the benefits our team identified as a result of choosing your attitude.

"First, by accepting that you choose tour attitude, you demonstrate a level of personal accountability and proactivity which will fill the third floor with energy, all by itself.

mutually exclusive 상호 배타적인 **accomplish** 성취하다 **animate** 생기 있
는 **compassionate** 인정 많은, 동정적인

"Second, choosing your attitude and acting like a victim are mutually exclusive."

"Third, we hope the attitude you choose is to bring your best self to work and so love to the work you do. We may not be able to do exactly what we love at the present time, but any of us can choose to love what we do. We can bring our best qualities to our work — it is our choice. If we can accomplish this one thing, our work area will become and oasis of energy. flexibility, and creativity in a tough industry."

Implementing Choose Your Attitude

Margaret, the highly animated team spokesperson, suggested that the implementation plan for Choose Your Attitude was a highly personal one. "Many of us have lost sight of our ability to choose. We must be compassionate with each other but work together to nurture our ability to exercise free will. If you don't believe you have choices or don't believe you have choices, you don't. There are people in our group who have had some very difficult life experiences. It will take some of us quite a while to be able to internalize this idea that we can choose our attitude."

surround 둘러싸다 **bitter** 고통스러운 **vital** 생명력 **extension** 확장

Another team member continued, "We have identified two ways to implement choose Your Attitude and have already taken some steps.

"First, we've purchased for everyone copies of a little book titled Personal Accountability: The Path to a Rewarding Work Life. Our group will organize discussion groups after you have had a chance to read it. If that goes well, we will follow with discussions of Raving Fans, the Seven Habits of Highly Effective People, Gung Ho!, and The Road Less Traveled. All of these books can help us understand the concept of choosing an attitude.

"Second, we've prepared an attitude menu for everyone to use back at the office. You've seen a version of this before. We still don't know who put the first one on our office door, so we can't give credit. Now you have your personal menu for each day."

Mary Jane looked down at her attitude menu. It had two sides. On one side was a frowning face surrounded by words like angry, disinterested, and bitter. On the other side was a smiling face with words like energetic, caring, vital, supportive, and creative. At the top it said: THE CHOICE IS YOURS. It was a nice extension of the menu over the main door to the third floor. Mart Jane jumped up

set off 기운차게 시작하다 congratulate 축하하다 stare 시선 regalia (정식
의)의복 lure 유혹하다 turn down 거절하다 luc-rative 유리한, 돈이 벌리는

• • •

Do you have a minute to talk?

잠시 이야기 할 시간이 있습니까?

전화상으로 상대방에게 잠간 이야기 할 시간을 내달라고 요청하는 공손한 표
현이다. 가까운 사이라면 "Got a minute?"이라고 간단하게 말해도 좋다.

and set off to congratulate each and every member of her staff with Lonnie a few steps behind her, providing his own brand of encouragement. It was after lunch before she finished talking with everyone. She now knew they were well on their way to cleaning up the toxic energy dump.

Lonnie walked Mary Jane back to First Guarantee. It wasn't surprising that they attracted a few stares: a businesswoman and a fishmonger in full regalia. What was surprising was how many knew Lonnie.

"So, your boss doesn' t know about the job offer, does he," said Lonnie. Two weeks earlier, Mary Jane had received an unexpected call from First Guarantee's main competitor, making and attempt to lure her away.

"I don't think so. I believe the recruiter talked to my old boss. The woman who recently left First Guarantee for a wonderful position in Portland. I haven't said anything at work."

"I couldn't understand your turning down such a lucrative offer, but now I see why. You are committed to this process, and you couldn't let these people down, could you?"

"That was part of it, Lonnie. But after working so hard to make First Guarantee more fun and a better place to work, why would I leave? The good times are just starting."

abundance 풍부함, 풍족함 **capable of** ~할 능력이 있는

• • •

This stuff is timeless. '이것(책 혹은 책의 내용)은 시간을 초월한다'

⟨3 **Sunday, February 7:** The Coffee Shop One Year Later

Mary Jane opened her book, *Simple Abundance*, and turned to February 7.

This stuff is timeless, she thought. A year ago I was sitting here, wondering how I would ever clean up the toxic energy dump. In fact, it was here that I realized I was part of the problem and needed to lead myself before I could lead the group.

Those committee reports at the hotel were a great start. The staff had always been capable of much more — it just

bring to light 끌어내다 **catch off guard** 허를 찌르다 **prominently** 두드러
지게, 현저히 **transcribe** 베끼다, 필기하다 **stumble across** 우연히 만나다
riddle 수수께끼

took some fish guys to bring those capabilities to light. The third floor is a different place now, and our new problem is all the people from around the company who want to work there. I guess the energy was there all the time.

And the Chairwoman's Award was such a nice surprise. I think the chairwoman was caught off guard when I asked for so many copies of the award. One for me, one for Bill, one for each employee in the department, and one for Lonnie and each of the other fish guys. I enjoy seeing it hanging above their cash register at the world famous Pike Place Fish market and displayed prominently in Lonnie's living room.

She opened her journal to one of her favorite selections she had transcribed, a piece written by John Gardner on the meaning in life.

Meaning

Meaning is not something you stumble across, like the answer to a riddle or the prize in a treasure hunt.

Meaning is something you build into your life.

affection 애정, 호의 **loyalty** 충성, 성실 **pass on** 지나가다 **be willing to** 기꺼이 ~하다 **sacrifice** 희생하다 **dignity** 위엄, 품위 **wipe** 닦다 **keeper** 파수꾼 **scone** 빵의 한 종류

· · ·

If it does, then the particular balance of success or failure is of less account '그렇게 한다면 성공 또는 실패의 상세한 평가는 별로 중요하지 않다' 여기서 'of less account'는 '별로 중요하지 않다'는 뜻의 숙어이다.

You build it out of your own past, out of your affections and loyalties, out of the experience of humankind as it is passed on to you, out of your own talent and understanding, out of the things you believe in, out of the things and people you love, out of the values for which you are willing to sacrifice something. The ingredients are there. You are the only one who can put them together into that pattern that will be your life. Let it be a life that has dignity and meaning for you. If it does, then the particular balance of success or failure is of less account.

— John Gardner

Mary Jane was wiping tears from her eyes as she closed the journal where she kept her thoughts and inspirational "keepers."

"Lonnie, could I have a piece of that scone, before you finish the whole darn thing?" Lonnie had been sitting quietly across from her, reading. He pushed the plate over to her. When she reached down for the scone, she found instead a small diamond engagement ring sitting in the large open mouth of a fish head. She looked up at Lonnie,

choking with laughter 웃음으로 숨이 막힌 채 **sputter** 흥분하며 말하다
ceremony 시상식 **podium** 연단, 연설대 **glance down** 흘끗 내려다보다
rediscover 재발견하다 **routine** 판에 박힌 일, 일상적인 일 **value-added** 부
가가치의

who had a large question mark on his nervous face. Choking with laughter, she sputtered, "Oh, Lonnie! Yes! Yes I will! But don't you ever stop playing?"

It had been a cold, dark, dreary day in Seattle on the outside. But something far different had been chosen for the inside.

THE CHAIRWOMAN'S AWARD CEREMONY

The chairwoman came to the podium and looked out at the audience. She glanced down at her notes and then looked up again saying, "I can't remember a prouder moment in my life than tonight. Something very special has happened at First Guarantee. In a back room operation on the third floor, Mary Jane Ramirez and her team members rediscovered that satisfying, rewarding work can be a choice we make when we come through the door in the morning. It is as simple as asking, 'Is this going to be a good day?' And answering, 'Yes! I choose to make this a great day!'

"Long-term employees have the enthusiasm of new hires and what was thought to be routine work has been transformed into value-added activity. I understand the

inscribe on ~위에 새기다 **plaque** 액자, 명판 **lapse** 착오, 실수 **surefire** 틀림없이 성공할, 실패하지 않는 **remedy** 치료, 구제

ingredients for this transformation were discovered at a local fish market. The team on the third floor observed that if you could make a fish market a great place to work, you could choose to make any department of First Guarantee a great place to work.

"The ingredients of this transformation are inscribed on a plaque which has been hung in the front entrance of our headquarters building. It reads as follows:

OUR WORKPLACE

As you enter this place of work please choose to make today a great day. Your colleagues, customers, team members, and you yourself will be thankful. Find ways to play. We can be serious about ourselves. Stay focused in order to be present when your customers and team members most need you. And should you feel your energy lapsing, try this surefire remedy: Find someone who needs a helping hand, a word of support, or a good eat—and make their day.

acknowledgment 감사의 글 single out 골라내다, 선발하다 recognition 인식, 인지 privilege 특권, 특전 awesome 아주 멋진 all-star cast 훌륭한 사람들이 총출동한 incredible 놀라운, 대단한 sustaining 지탱하는, 유지하는

Acknowledgments

There are many who have worked to make this book a success and we want to recognize them all, fully knowing we will probably miss someone, Fist we will acknowledge the special people and then single out four for extra recognition.

You couldn' t ask for a better publisher. It seems unfair to the industry that Hyperion should have so much superior talent. Included on the fantastic team with whom we had the privilege to work are:

Bob Miller, Martha Levin, Ellen Archer, Jane Comins, Michael Burkin, Mark Chait, Jennifer landers. Claire Ellis, Andrea Ho, David Lott, Vincent Stanley, and thanks also to the awesome Time-Warner Trade Publishing sales force.

And how did we get so lucky as to find the world's best agency? The Margret McBride Agency includes an all-star cast: Jason Cabbssi, Donna DeGutis, Sangeeta Mehta, Kris Sauer.

There would not be a book if it weren't for the incredible Pike Place Fish. Thanks to johnny Yokoyama, the owner, and the amazing fish guys for creating and sustaining a would famous fish market.

accomplish 성취하다 individual 개인 Mobius-Award 유명한 국제 광고제 중 하나 guidance 안내

· · ·

...many little gesture that add up to a whole lot of help '많은 힘이 된 수많은 작은 도움들'

And then there are the accomplished authors and business leaders who have shared their wisdom and their words. It is such an honor to have these talented individuals offering their support: Sheldon Bowles, Richard Chang, Peter Economy, Peter Isler, Spencer Johnson, Lori Lockhart, Bob Nelson, Robert J. Nugent, Hyrum Smith, Donald D. Snyder, Richard Sulpizio.

We want to thank the employees of The Ken Blanchard Companies and ChartHouse Learning for the many little gestures that add up to a whole lot of help.

And we would like to recognize four people who made major contributions: Our editor, Will Schwalbe, brought enthusiasm, experience, and a willingness always to be looking for ways to improve the book, right down to the last minute.

Patrick North of ChartHouse offered his Mobius Award-winning talent.

Ken Blanchard offered his guidance and wrote a wonderful foreword.

Finally, the agent of all agents, Margret McBride. For a writer, she is a treasure.

Thanks.

Stephen C. Lundin, Harry Paul, and John Christensen

펄떡이는
물고기처럼
〈한글 요약문〉

시애틀 월요일 아침

메리 제인 라미레즈는 3년 전, 따뜻한 남캘리포니아에서 시애틀로 이사를 왔다. 남편의 새로운 직장 때문이었는데 제인도 시애틀로 온 뒤 '제일보증 금융회사'라는 좋은 직장에 취직할 수 있었다. 하지만 시애틀로 이사한 지 12개월 만에 남편 댄이 동맥류 파열로 인해 쓰러졌다. 남편과 작별인사도 하지 못한 채 영원히 이별하게 된 것이다.

제일 보증 금융회사에서 일한 지난 3년 동안 메리 제인은 '무슨 일이든 해내고 마는 관리자'라는 좋은 평판을 얻었다. 그녀는 언제나 자신의 업무를 정해진 시간 안에, 그것도 가장 높은 품질로 완수했기 때문에 다른 부서의 사람들이 언제나 그녀의 부서를 거쳐 일을 진행하려고 했다. 또한 부하직원들에게 함께 일하고 싶은 가장 좋은 상사로 꼽혔다. 수평적이며 자유로운 토의를 이끌어내는 리더십으로 부하직원들의 존경과 호감을 불러일으켰으며, 부장으로서 부서의 생산성을 향상시켰기 때문이다. 결국 그녀의 팀은 3년 만에 '믿을 수 있는 팀'이라는 명성을 얻게 됐다.

이 회사에는 제인의 부서와 대조적인 부서가 있다. 회사 건물 3층에 있는 규모가 제법 큰 관리부서로 이 부서는 주로 '둔감하고 게으르며 불쾌하다는 부정적인 평가를 받고 있었다. 회사의 모든 업무가 이 부서를 거쳐 갔기 때문에 이 부서에 대한 이야기는 언제나 사람들이 입에 오르내렸다. 그런데 제인이 바로 이 부서의 부장으로 승진하게 된 것이다. 제인은 처음에는 좀 망설였지만 다달이 갚아 나가는 남편의 병원비를 생각하니 도저히 거절할 수가 없었다.

새로운 부서로 발령을 받고 첫 5주 동안, 제인은 새로운 업무와 동료들을 이해하기 위해 노력했다. 이 부서의 사람들은 대부분 다 좋은 사람들이었다. 하지만 제인은 곧 이 부서가 왜 그런 명성을 얻게 되었는지 이해할 수 있었다. 직원들은 서류작업을 재촉하는 다른 부서의 직원들을 피하기 위해 전화도 받지 않았으며, 휴게실에서 졸고 있기 일쑤이거나 변명만 늘어놓았다. 제인은 어디서부터 시작해야 할지 몰라 절망감에 사로잡혔다.

어느 날 제인은 자신의 상사인 빌에게서 전화를 받았다. 이사회의에서 회사의 가장 큰 문제로 3층 부서가 지목되었다는 내용이었다. 심지어 회장은 3층 부서를 '유독성 폐기물 더미'라고 불렀다고 했다. 제인은 자신의 부서를 어떻게 변화시켜야 할지 심각하게 고민했다.

세계적인 파이크 플레이스 어시장

어느 점심시간, 부둣가를 거닐다가 제인은 우연히 근처의 파이크 플레이스 어시장에 들어서게 됐다. 그리고 제인은 그곳에서 놀라운 광경을 보게 된다. 상인들이 커다란 생선을 공중으로 던지며 큰 목소리로 "연어 한 마리 미네소타로 날아갑니다" 등의 말들을 외치고 있었다. 그리고 손에 요구르트를 든 많은 회사원들이 그 광경을 구경하고 있었다. 그곳의 에너지는 남달랐다.

모두들 바다의 표면 위를 박차고 뛰어 오르는 생동감 넘치는 싱싱한 물고기처럼 보였다.

여기서 제인은 시장 상인인 로니를 만났다. 로니는 정신없는 와중에서도 제인의 고민을 들어주었다. 그리고 그 고민을 해결하도록 도와주겠다는 제안을 했다. 제인은 그들의 만남에서 다음과 같은 교훈을 얻었다.

'비록 당신이 어떤 일을 하는가에는 선택의 여지가 없다 하더라도, 당신이 어떤 방법으로 그 일을 할 것인가에 대해서는 항상 선택의 여지가 있다', '직업을 대하는 태도는 우리가 선택한다!'

나의 하루를 선택하기

제인은 로니에게 '왜 어떤 일을 하는가에 대한 선택의 여지가 없는지' 물었다. 로니는 이에 '언제라도 직장을 그만둘 수 있고, 그런 의미에서 일을 선택할 수 있지만 자신이 책임져야 할 여러 가지 요소들을 고려할 때 현명한 결정이 아닐 수 있기 때문'이라고 말했다. 하지만 매일 직장으로 출근하면서 취할 수 있는 태도는 무궁무진하다는 것이다. 로니 자신은 수산시장에서 일하는 것이 힘들지만 기왕이면 '제일 좋은 날'을 만들자고 결정한다고 했다.

'매일 일터로 가져오는 태도를 선택한다. 그 선택은 일하는 방법을 결정한다'

제인은 변화를 위해 우선 회장님이 들었다는 세미나에 관한 정보를 얻고자 했다. 이를 위해 제인은 그녀의 상사인 빌에게 전화를 걸어 정보를 부탁했다. 그런데 빌은 시간 낭비한다며 제인에게 핀잔을 주었다. 하지만 제인은 이에 주눅 들지 않고 빌에게 협조를 요구했고 회장님이 들었다는 세미나의 테이프를 얻을 수 있었다.

제인은 테이프를 얻은 날 퇴근길에 자신의 상사 빌과의 대화를 생각했다. 그리고 자신이 상사에게 용감하게 하고 싶은 말은 한 것이 2년 만이라는 사실을 깨달았다. '왜 그렇게 되었을까'를 고민하다가 제인은 세미나 테이프를 틀었다. 테이프에서는 데이비드 화이트의 '믿음'이라는 시가 흘러나왔다. 제인은 그것을 들었을 때 감동을 주체할 수 없었다. '학생이 준비되었을 때 스승이 나타난다'는 말이 이런 것이구나! 제인은 2년 동안 자신이 자신감을 잃었던 이유를 알게 되었다. 그녀는 남편의 갑작스런 죽음으로 인해 혼자 세상에 남겨진 자신의 능력에 대한 믿음을 잃었던 것이다. 또한 그녀가 실패한다면 자신과 두 아이의 삶

에 위기가 오기 때문에 변화를 두려워했던 것이다. 하지만 이제
는 변화하지 않으면 오히려 직장을 잃을 수도 있는 상황이 되었
다. 그리고 그녀는 더 이상 에너지와 생명이 없는 곳에서 일하고
싶지 않았다.

제인은 자신만을 위한 일요일 오후에 사라 밴 브라낙스의《단
순한 풍요로움》과 존 가드너의 연설문을 읽으며 생각을 정리했
다. 그녀는 진정한 리더가 되기 위해서는 위험부담을 감수해야
한다고 생각했다. 그리고 변화의 첫 단계로 자신의 태도를 선택
하기로 했다. 그녀는 자신감, 확신, 그리고 믿음을 선택했다.

그녀는 자신의 선택을 실천에 옮기기로 했다. 회의를 소집해
서 직원들에게 '삶의 태도를 선택한다'는 개념을 이해하게 하고
동기부여를 하고자 했다.

그녀는 직원들에게 3층 부서에 대한 평판과 회장님의 견해를
이야기했다. 직원들은 모두 놀라고 당황한 모습이 역력했다. 그
리고 자신들에 대한 평판에 불만을 토로했다. 하지만 부서에 활
기와 생동감이 없다는 비난에 대해서 이의를 제기하는 사람은
아무도 없었다. 스티브라는 직원은 '우리 중 누군가가 변화하기
를 거부한다 해도 포기하지 말라'며 그녀를 격려하기도 했다.
회의가 있던 주의 금요일에는 놀라운 일이 벌어졌다. 어떤 직원

이 사무실 앞에 '당신의 하루를 선택하십시오!'라는 제목의 포스터를 붙여 놓은 것이다. 제인은 직원들이 '이제 이해하기 시작했구나'라는 생각에 감동했다.

토요일 아침에 제인은 아이들과 함께 로니를 만나러 어시장으로 갔다. 그녀의 아들 브래드는 로니의 일을 도우면서 최고의 시간을 보냈다.

놀이 찾기

제인은 로니와 브래드를 보면서 삶의 태도를 선택한 사람들이 실천해야 하는 두 번째 요소를 알게 되었다. 바로 '놀이'였다. 업무를 처리하는 방식에서 즐거움을 찾고, 고객을 존중하는 마음을 가지고 그들이 재미를 느끼도록 아이들처럼 노는 것이다.

그들의 날 만들어주기

로니는 제인에게 어시장에서 가장 인상적이었던 것이 무엇이었냐고 물었다. 그녀는 한 아가씨가 직접 생선을 잡아보려고 노력하던 모습이라고 대답했다. 그녀는 그 모습에서 활기와 즐거움을 느꼈다. 어시장 사람들은 그것을 '그들의 날 만들어주기'라고 불렀다. 어시장을 방문한 사람들에게 기억에 남을 만한 추억거리를 만들어주고, 고객들을 '참여시키는' 것이다. 제인은 '다른 사람의 날을 만들어 주려는 데 주의를 집중하는 것은 지속적이고 긍정적인 감정의 흐름을 제공하게 된다'는 것을 깨달았다.

그 자리에 있기

제인은 어시장을 주의 깊게 살펴보면서 그곳의 또 다른 비결 하나를 찾아냈다. 그것은 상인들이 한 순간도 쉬지 않고 고객을 바라본다는 것이었다. 어시장의 상인들은 고객을 기쁘게 하기 위해 항상 그 자리에서 그들과 함께 했다.

일요일 오후

'나의 하루를 선택하기, 놀이 찾기, 그들의 날 만들어 주기, 그 자리에 있기'라는 피시 철학의 4가지 요소를 깨달은 제인은 월요일 아침 회의에서 직원들에게 어시장을 견학할 것을 제안했다. 사람들은 불평했지만 제인은 다시 한 번 강력하게 제안했다.

어시장을 방문한 첫 번째 그룹은 주의 깊게 어시장을 관찰하고 상인들과 대화를 나눴다. 두 번째 그룹은 첫 번째 그룹에게서 이야기를 많이 들어서인지 처음에는 소극적인 태도를 보였다. 그때 특별한 일이 일어났다. 한 상인이 얌전하기로 유명한 스테파니를 카운터 위로 불러 올렸던 것이다. 스테파니는 처음에는 주저했지만 주변의 성화에 카운터로 올라갔다. 그리고 세 번째 시도에서 생선을 멋지게 받아내 그곳에 있던 사람들의 환호를 받았다. 이 사건을 계기로 사람들은 어시장의 분위기에 적응하기 시작했다.

금요일 오후에 제인은 두 그룹과 각각 회의를 가졌다. 사람들은 저마다 어시장에 대한 소감을 이야기했고 변화의 필요성을 털어 놓았다. 그들은 삶에 대한 태도를 선택할 수 있다는 것을 이해하게 된 것이다. 그들은 피시 철학을 부서에 실제로 적용하기 위한 아이디어를 모으기로 했다. 이것이 직원들에게 주말 동안의 숙제로 주어졌다.

직원들 중 여섯 명이나 주말에 어시장을 다시 방문했다. 그들은 각자 피시 철학의 4가지 요소에 대해 상인들에게 질문하고 대화를 나누었다. 또 다시 어시장을 방문한 다른 동료들을 보고

다시 한 번 변화의 의지를 다지게 됐다.

월요일 아침 회의에서 직원들은 어시장에서 배운 교훈들에 대해 이야기했다. 자신의 개인적인 아픔과 깨달음을 털어 놓는 직원들도 있었다. 직원들은 이제 다음 단계로 나아가기 위한 아이디어들을 내놓았다. 4개의 팀을 구성해 피시 철학의 4가지 요소들을 각각 맡아 발표하는 것으로 의견이 모아졌다. 각 팀들은 6주 동안 프레젠테이션을 준비하기로 했고 프레젠테이션에는 행동 지침들을 포함하기로 했다.

᠕ᢒ 팀 보고회

놀이 찾기 팀

이 팀은 게임 형식으로 프레젠테이션을 준비했다. 다른 직원들이 게임을 통해 '놀이가 주는 좋은 점'과 '우리 부서에서 놀이를 어떻게 실천할 수 있을까?' 에 관한 내용들을 알아갈 수 있었다.

그들의 날 만들어주기 팀

이 팀은 다른 직원들을 소그룹으로 나누고 내부 고객인 직원들의 업무를 지지하고 후원하기 위한 전략을 세워볼 것을 먼저 요구했다. 그리고 그들은 '고객 여론조사' 결과를 발표했다. 그 내용은 충격적인 것이었다. 직원들은 남은 시간 동안 고객 여론조사를 통해 드러난 문제를 해결하기 위해 열정적으로 토의했고 가장 훌륭한 아이디어를 제시한 4번 팀에게 상을 주었다. '4번 팀의 날'을 만들어준 것이다.

그 자리에 있기 팀

이 팀은 전혀 새로운 시도를 했다. '과거는 역사입니다, 미래는 신비입니다, 오늘은 선물입니다, 그래서 우리는 현재를 선물이라고 부릅니다'라는 시를 읽어주고는 존이라는 직원이 자신의 이야기를 털어 놓았다. 그는 딸아이에게 아빠로서 곁에 있어주지 못했던 자신의 과거 이야기를 하고, 딸에게 용서를 구하고 딸 곁에 있어주기로 한 자신의 변화에 대해 이야기했다. 그리고 직원들은 고객들 또는 같이 일하는 다른 사람들을 위해 그 자리에 있기 위한 방법을 고안해냈다.

태도 선택 팀

이 팀은 '태도 선택의 장점'과 '태도 선택의 실행 방법'에 대해 단도직입적으로 프레젠테이션을 했다. 또 태도 선택을 실행에 옮길 수 있는 첫 번째 방법으로 관련 책을 함께 읽고 토의하는 방법을 제안했다. 그리고 두 번째 방법으로 개개인의 태도 메뉴판을 만들어 나누어 주었다.

이제 제일금융의 3층 부서 사람들에게는 가장 일하기 좋은 일터에서의 즐거운 시간들이 기다리고 있었다.

그로부터 1년 후

피시 철학을 3층 부서에 성공적으로 도입한 제인은 회장상을 수상하게 됐다. 그녀는 수상 연설로 다음과 같은 말은 했다.

"우리는 매일 아침 사무실에 들어서면서 만족과 보상을 제공하는 일터를 갖기로 선택할 수 있다는 사실을 재발견했습니다. 그것은 바로 '오늘 하루는 좋은 날이 될 것인가'라고 묻고, 거기에 대해 '그래! 난 오늘 하루를 멋진 날로 만들겠어!'라고 대답하는, 어찌 보면 매우 단순한 작업입니다. 하지만 이런 활동을 통해 관리부서의 전 직원들은 모두 신입사원들과 같은 열성을 갖게 되었고 습관적이었던 업무는 가치가 부여된 활동들로 탈바꿈하였습니다."

Authors

STEPHEN C. LUNDIN, PH.D., is a filmmaker, graduate business school professor, and professional speaker. He runs a corporate membership seminar series as part of the Institute for Management Studies and leads the Institute for Creativity and Innovation at the University of St. Thomas in Minneapolis.

HARRY PAUL is currently a senior vice president with The Ken Blanchard Companies, where he coordinates special projects and manages their internal speakers bureau. He lives in California.

JOHN CHRISTENSEN, an award-winning filmmaker, lives in Minneapolis. He is now CEO of ChartHouse Learning Corporation, the leading producer of corporate learning films, including Fish!, the video, which has been adopted by thousands of corporations nationwide.

bureau (관청의)국 **adopt** 채택하다 **nationwide** 전국적인, 전국적으로

해설 유동익

아주대학교 대학원에서 영문학석사, 명지대학교 대학원에서 영문학박사 학위를 받았으며 미국 프린스턴 대학교에서 연구 활동을 했다. 명지대학교, 수원여자대학교, 장안대학 등에서 강의를 했으며, 현재는 전문 번역가로 활동 중이다. 저서로는《한 번만 읽으면 확 잡히는 중학교 영어》,《한 번만 읽으면 확 잡히는 고등학교 영어》가 있다.

한언의 사명선언문

Since 3rd day of January, 1998

Our Mission — · 우리는 새로운 지식을 창출, 전파하여 전 인류가 이를 공유케
함으로써 인류문화의 발전과 행복에 이바지한다.

— · 우리는 끊임없이 학습하는 조직으로서 자신과 조직의 발전
을 위해 쉼없이 노력하며, 궁극적으로는 세계적 컨텐츠 그룹
을 지향한다.

— · 우리는 정신적, 물질적으로 최고 수준의 복지를 실현하기 위
해 노력하며, 명실공히 초일류 사원들의 집합체로서 부끄럼없
이 행동한다.

Our Vision 한언은 컨텐츠 기업의 선도적 성공모델이 된다.

저희 한언인들은 위와 같은 사명을 항상 가슴 속에 간직하고
좋은 책을 만들기 위해 최선을 다하고 있습니다.
독자 여러분의 아낌없는 충고와 격려를 부탁드립니다.

· 한언 가족 ·

HanEon's Mission statement

Our Mission — · We create and broadcast new knowledge for the
advancement and happiness of the whole human
race.

— · We do our best to improve ourselves and the
organization, with the ultimate goal of striving to
be the best content group in the world.

— · We try to realize the highest quality of welfare
system in both mental and physical ways and we
behave in a manner that reflects our mission as
proud members of HanEon Community.

Our Vision HanEon will be the leading Success Model of the
content group.